FULL THROTTLE

122 STRATEGIES TO SUPERCHARGE YOUR PERFORMANCE AT WORK

GREGG M. STEINBERG, PhD

WILEY

John Wiley & Sons, Inc.

Published by John Wiley & Sons, Inc., Hoboken, New Jersey.

Published simultaneously in Canada.

For general information on our other products and services or for technical support, please contact our Customer Care Department within the United States at (800) 762-2974, outside the United States at (317) 572-3993 or fax (317) 572-4002.

Wiley also publishes its books in a variety of electronic formats. Some content that appears in print may not be available in electronic books. For more information about Wiley products, visit our web site at www.wiley.com.

Library of Congress Cataloging-in-Publication Data:

Steinberg, Gregg M., 1963-
    Full throttle: 122 strategies to supercharge your performance at work/by Gregg M. Steinberg.
        p. cm.
    Includes bibliographical references.
    ISBN 978-0-470-45242-4 (cloth)
1. Success in business. 2. Performance. 3. Performance—Psychological aspects. 4. Employee motivation. I. Title.
    HF5386.S856 2009
    650.1—dc22

                                        2008054904

Printed in the United States of America

10 9 8 7 6 5 4 3 2 1

CONTENTS

ACKNOWLEDGMENTS

There are many people who contributed to the making of this book. I first want to thank Shannon Vargo, Editor at Wiley, for her vision of this book and continual support of my work. Her kind words will always be appreciated. I also want to thank the team at Wiley: Deborah Schindlar, Senior Production Editor, and Beth Zipko, Editorial Assistant, for helping turn the book into a reality. I also want to thank all the people I have worked with who have inspired me to share their stories and helpful hints with a bigger audience. I also want to thank my friends—Barbara Barna, Charlie Nickell, David Meador, Rudy Kalis, Clarence Quillen, Craig Patrick, Teresa Shiping, Mark Moore, Stan Morrison, Mark Harmon, and Dewey Bushaw—who shared with me some great stories that I've used in this book.

I also want to thank Bea Steinberg for all her thoughtful advice and words of encouragement, which helped make this a better book. Lastly, I want to thank Tommie Kay for her love and support.

INTRODUCTION

Master Your Emotions—Master Your World

Mastering our emotions is the X-factor to success. I discovered this performance principle to my own demise on the golf course more than 20 years ago.

The place was the Calabasas Country Club, site of the U.S. amateur qualifier. At this site, they were going to take only one person to go to Pebble Beach, my favorite place on the planet. I was only a high school senior at the time, and I knew I was out of my league, about to compete against some of the best college players in Southern California. But I thought, what the heck, it was the U.S. Amateur at Pebble Beach. I had to go for it.

Let us fast forward this story to the eighteenth tee. Amazingly, unbelievably, I was in the lead. My playing partner was Mighty John, six feet, three inches, and the current Number One player at UCLA and he was two strokes behind me, and the rest of the field was three strokes behind him.

The eighteenth hole was a 510-yard, par 5, slight dogleg right. But I was not thinking about par; I was in the Zone. For the previous holes, when I looked down the fairways, all I could see was open space. I had no thoughts of where the trouble was on the hole—there were no water hazards or out-of-bounds, just the safety of the fairway. When I looked at the greens, all I could see was the flag-stick. When I got to the green, the hole looked huge, like a 10-foot round circle. Everything was going in—10-footers, 20-footers—everything. I was calm and completely confident in my game. I felt invincible.

As I was about to hit my last tee shot of the day, I did my wiggles and waggles, and then suddenly heard, "Wait, wait . . . someone is driving up the fairway." Someone was indeed driving up the fairway—it was my little brother Jake. And he was going as fast as he could. He pulled up to the tee box and yelled, slightly out of breath, "Gregg, Gregg, if you par this hole, we are going to Pebble Beach."

Now my thoughts shifted in reverse—I thought par, Pebble Beach, par, all I needed was a par. The feeling was as if a two-by-four piece of wood had slammed across my head. My hands instantly became all sweaty; my heart started to jump out of my chest; my ears began to tingle and my eyesight began to go in and out of focus. I thought I still need to hit this tee ball, so I got up to my ball, did my wiggles and waggles again, and then topped my tee shot 70 yards into the weeds up ahead.

After 3 minutes and 59 seconds, we found my ball and I took a mighty swipe with my 7-iron. Now, I was 30 yards behind Mighty John, who had just hit a 300-yard drive. I got up to my ball and smashed a 3-wood, just on the fringe short of the green. Mighty John got up to his ball, and coolly and calmly hit his 3-iron to 40 feet from the pin.

As we walked up the green, there were about 100 people waiting for us. They all knew one of us was going to make it to Pebble Beach. I could feel their eyes piercing my skin. My mind now began to race faster and faster. All I could think was, "Don't leave this putt short; don't leave it right; get it to the hole, you idiot." Bam—I hit my putt 10 feet by the hole. Then Mighty John got up to his ball and again coolly and calmly rolled it in for an eagle. We were tied at that moment.

I then got over to my 10-footer and thought, "All you have to do is make this for par and we are in the playoff. Don't leave it short, don't leave it right." I left my ball five inches short of the cup.

Mighty John went to Pebble Beach that summer and I got to sit at home with my little brother Jake.

That was the bad news.

The good news is that day I vowed to understand why some people choke under pressure like I did, and why some people excel under pressure like Mighty John. I have written this book to share with you my years of knowledge—what I have learned as a sport psychology consultant to many professional athletes, as a performance coach to business-people, as well as my own research.

All my experiences have led to one undeniable truth: When you master your emotions, you master your world. Emotional control is the essential ingredient to our health, happiness, and productivity. Yes, mental toughness is vital and our thinking can help to guide our emotions, but ulti-mately, it is our emotions that control our performance. Emotions drive the engine down the path to failure or suc-cess. When you are consumed by the fear of losing your job, mad at your boss, or stuck in a joyless job, then your potential is drained and your performance will suffer. On the other hand, when you feel jazzed to be at work, see the stress of the situation as an enjoyable challenge, and truly like your job, then your talents will be unleashed and you will soar. Regardless of venue, this principle is woven into the fabric of success. Whether you are a CEO, a world-class athlete, salesperson, or secretary—your emotions control your destiny.

The importance of emotional mastery leading to a pros-perous life is not a new belief. The ancient Greeks used the term *sophrosyne* to describe the ability to value fortune and disaster in the same light. They believed qualities such as self-mastery and self-control would transcend time as essentials for a prosperous life. Today, we know that success lies not so much in ability but in emotional intelligence. Popularized by Daniel Goleman, emotional intelligence has been accepted as an essential ingredient to success and happiness in the new age.

Full Throttle takes emotional mastery one step further. *Full Throttle* introduces emotional mastery through the development of our emotional strengths. As with our physical strengths and fitness, we must maintain and build our emotional strengths. The greater we can develop our emotional strengths, the greater is our emotional control over our world, and ultimately, the greater the chance for happiness and prosperity.

To explain how these six emotional strengths interact, picture yourself on a journey to the top of a mountain. We are all on this climb toward excellence, whether it is to win a championship, be promoted to the corner office, or to have a happy and fulfilling life. The following six emotional strengths will help you achieve your goals.

1. *Emotional Awareness:* This is your road map. You must be aware of which emotions energize you and which drain you. When you understand when your energies peak, you can capitalize on those periods. You also need to know when it's time to recharge and refuel.

2. *Emotional Preparedness:* Events rarely go as planned. You must be emotionally ready for any difficulties that may arise. To be successful, you need to plan for the best, but prepare for the worst. Bad events will not drain your energies when you're ready for them.

3. *Emotional Bravado:* Fear creates negative energy, which can block your journey or, at least, slow you down. Winners channel the negative energy of fear into a positive action, an opportunity to grow.

4. *Emotional Connectedness:* We must be fully connected to the moment, or we may get lost on our journey. Successful individuals focus their energies in the here and now. Once we are fully engaged in the present, our life gets that much sweeter.

5. *Emotional Drive:* To reach the top in any field, knowledge is not enough and intention is not enough. To get results, we must be proactive and take action. But action requires boundless energy and a committed heart.

6. *Emotional Balance:* Success is a long journey. It will take much more than winning to sustain our hunger. We need balance as well as meaning and purpose to make this long trek to the top.

These six emotional strengths create the sections for the book. While these sources are interconnected, they are interdependent. You must master all six to fully ignite your energy and master your emotions. Readers can turn, however, to any section they believe is most needed at that time. The Emotional Strength Assessment Tool (ESAT) is provided in the last chapter of this book. The ESAT is a paper-and-pencil assessment that measures all six emotional strengths in about 10 minutes.

Sections are composed of a series of short and entertaining chapters. An ancient proverb states, "Tell me a fact and I'll learn. Tell me the truth and I will believe. But tell me a story and it will live in my heart forever." Each chapter begins with a success story of some athlete or business executive I have coached, or with a story about a high-achieving individual that I want to share with you. I believe if we understand how Tiger Woods, Bill Gates, or Rudy Giuliani have gained emotional mastery, then we will gain the competitive edge needed to thrive in our lives.

Each chapter concludes with usable activities and important tips that will allow you to capitalize in any setting.

Because busy people want to make good use of their time, the activities are streamlined for the fast pace of today's world. For example, the drill "Snap out of it!" shows you how to channel negative thoughts into a positive source of energy in a few brief moments. In all, there are 122 quick and effective drills to recharge, refuel, and refocus your life.

Full Throttle gives you a coherent and enduring system that, if practiced, moves you toward a better way to live. If you choose to thrive on the inside, this book is your guide.

PART I

EMOTIONAL AWARENESS

First and foremost, champions know who they are and what makes them tick. They know what emotions drive their engine. They know when they peak in their energies and how to harness that power. Winners like Lance Armstrong develop plans to harness their strengths to be successful. Champions like Tony Gwynn understand what got them there, and at times, go back to the basics to get back to the top of their games. Emotional awareness can help you develop a road map that guides your life journey.

Do you know your energy cycles? Are you aware of your strengths and true talents? Do you know what gets you in the flow and what causes you to choke?

The following section shows you how to find your flow as well as helps you develop a vision based upon the principles of self-awareness. Once you have a plan based on your true self, the steps of the journey are easy.

CHAPTER ONE

Cycling with Energy

Place two fingers on the side of your neck and get your pulse. Did you feel the rhythm of your beating heart? This is the rhythm of life.

This rhythm is within us and all around us—the ebb and flow of tides, the migration of the birds, the moon orbiting the Earth, and the Earth orbiting the Sun. There is a heartbeat to the Universe.

Thomas Edison had the pulse of the inventing world at the turn of the twentieth century. He was renowned for his incredible output (1,093 patents) and work ethic. It is believed that he would work for days without sleep—but that is a myth.

The truth is that Edison knew his internal rhythms—he was aware of his working cycle and used this to his advantage. Edison was a notorious nap taker. He would crawl up on his desk and use his favorite chemistry books as pillows. He allowed himself time to re-throttle. Edison knew he needed time to rejuvenate his body and his mind for the incredible work that lay ahead.

Some people lack the intuitive sense of internal rhythms that Edison had. They just run hard and fast instead, believing that if they do not, the competition will pass them by. Tim Howard, a sales executive, had this problem. He would schedule as many appointments as he could in a day. While Tim was moderately successful, he felt his biggest problem was his inability to connect with many of his clients.

As he and I worked together on this problem, we discovered that Tim was scheduling important clients when he was naturally cycling down in his energy—Tim was trying to go full-throttle when he should have been re-throttling in his energy levels. As a result, he was faking his energy during important client meetings, which made his actions look faked and forced. His clients read those subtle clues as a form of distrust, decreasing his chances of a successful interaction.

To turn Tim's business around, we created a plan that allowed him to become more aware of his energy cycles. The plan also helped Tim match his important activities to the appropriate times in his day. When this occurred, he exuded positive energy at the correct times, which helped him develop a greater connection to his clients.

Knowing when to go full-throttle and when to re-throttle will be a significant key to your longevity as well as success in the world of business. The following drills help to capitalize on your energy cycles using a three-step energy management plan.

FIRST STEP: DISCOVER YOUR CYCLES

Dr. Richard Carlson wrote many self-help books, including the best-selling *Don't Sweat the Small Stuff*. He wrote only very early in the morning, when he was peaking in his creative energy. While he accomplished many tasks during the day as a psychologist, consultant, and speaker, Carlson learned that the crack of dawn was his best time to fulfill his destiny as a writer.

To maximize productivity, you must first pay attention to the rising and falling of your energy cycles. Does your energy soar in the morning? Does it take a skid after lunch? Do you have a second wind in the evening? Awareness of your energy is the first step to harnessing it.

To accomplish this task, develop a scale that rates your energy. Allow the number zero on the scale to signify a period when you have very little energy. Mark 100 on the scale to indicate when you are completely revved up with great energy. Mark your scale in 10-point increments, describing each incremental step with a simple sentence such as "moderate energy" or "good energy."

Next, rate your energy levels in two-hour blocks for each day (See Table 1.1, Step 2). Do this for one week. For instance, you may find your energy peaks from 8:00 to 10:00 in the morning. You then take a bit of a slide in the mid-morning, and then peak after lunch only to discover another slide around 3 P.M. Or, you may find that you are revved up in the afternoon, but percolate with a bit of energy only in the morning hours.

While most individuals will have a few peaks and valleys throughout the day, everyone is unique. Knowing when your energy soars as well as when it droops is the first step in learning to harness it.

SECOND STEP: CREATE AN ENERGY LIST

Most successful individuals create a to-do list. They may create this list before they leave work, and these tasks relate to what will be accomplished the following day. Or, they may create their list as the day's first task.

Try something new: create an energy to-do list. Quantify each activity on the list in terms of three different levels of energy: high, moderate, and low. (See Table 1.1) As an

Table 1.1 Energy To-do List

STEP 1: DISCOVER YOUR CYCLES

Rank 10–100 (in 10-point increments)

	Mon	**Tues**	**Wed**	**Thurs**	**Fri**
8–10					
10–12					
12–2					
2–4					
4–6					

STEP 2: CREATE AN ENERGY LIST

High energy tasks:

Moderate energy tasks:

Low energy tasks:

STEP 3: MATCH YOUR TASKS

	Mon	**Tues**	**Wed**	**Thurs**	**Fri**
8–10					
10–12					
12–2					
2–4					
4–6					

example, meeting an important client for the first time can require a vast amount of energy. Meeting with a disgruntled client and resolving a key issue can be very draining as well. On the other hand, making cold calls, or writing a proposal require moderate energy; simple analysis and warm calls can be low-energy tasks.

THIRD STEP: MATCH YOUR TASKS

The third step of the plan is to schedule your tasks for the appropriate time of day. Based upon the previous two steps, place the most demanding energy tasks in the times when you have the most energy. Position moderate energy tasks for when you begin to slide in your energy. Do low energy tasks when your energy levels have bottomed out.

Your peak energy periods are precious. Safeguard them for the demanding activities that will be most profitable to you. Save the tasks that require very little mental and emotional energy for the times when you begin to slide. You can still be highly effective if you accomplish simple tasks during your low-energy periods.

Knowing when to sprint and when to slow your pace will help you finish the day with a quantity of accomplishments.

READJUSTING YOUR PEAK PERIODS

An important question I receive at many seminars is whether you can readjust the timing of your peak periods. The answer is yes!

Antonio Ravette, a concert violinist, would get up early in the morning, around 6:30 A.M. But after the analysis we discussed earlier, we discovered that he peaked at 9 A.M. and again at 3 P.M. Antonio had recently been hired by the Nashville Symphony, which usually starts their performances at 7 P.M. at the Shimmerhorn Concert Hall. To remedy this issue, we had Antonio sleep until 9:30 A.M. That pushed his cycles to peak three hours later—to a time when he needed to be surging in his energy cycles.

If you need to readjust your cycles, perhaps sleeping a little later may do your energy some good.

CHAPTER TWO

Vision Guides Destiny

Driving to spring training in Florida, the famous baseball player and New York Yankees manager, Yogi Berra, and his wife were terribly late. They were driving all night and Yogi's wife fell fast asleep. To make up for lost time, Yogi took a short cut that eventually turned into a dirt road with more dirt than road. His wife suddenly awoke, very startled, and said to Yogi, "Honey, I think we're lost." Yogi, always ready with a quick quip, replied, "Yeah but we're making great time."

Without vision, you may get somewhere, but most likely it will be the somewhere you don't want. Vision guides your destiny. It did for Gary Player. As a young lad growing up in South Africa, Gary had the vision of his greatness. Gary would stand in front of a mirror and say over and over "You are going to be one of the greatest players of all time." Gary Player's vision shined very brightly, and guided him to become one of the greatest golfers of the twentieth century.

Vision can create our end point even if one does not currently exist. When Tommy Burnett entered the University of Virginia in 1993, he declared to his professor that his vision was to be a special effects expert on a *Star Wars* movie. Unfortunately for him, the last *Star Wars* movie had been made 10 years earlier.

Given that predicament, most people would choose another direction. Not Tommy. He had a vision of bringing to life his favorite science fiction characters on the silver screen and making them appear real. He read everything he could get his hands on regarding how to create special effects and how to program these effects. He became an expert on a new computer programming language called Python.

Fortunately, Industrial Light & Magic, the company owned by George Lucas and creator of the *Star Wars* movies, needed someone who knew Python. Tommy was their man and was hired to develop special effects for the new *Star Wars* movies in 1999, 2002, and 2003. Tommy's vision created his destiny.

Our vision is our light. We all need this light. In a sense, it is a survival mechanism. Psychologists discovered that when mice were placed in a tub with no way out, they would stop swimming after 45 minutes and drown. However, if the mice had a light shining upon them, they would continue to swim for 36 hours. The mice were motivated through the darkness by a vision of light.

Vision guided Christopher Reeve throughout his darkest hours—his vision was the light at the end of his tragic tunnel. Christopher Reeve's rise to fame was fierce, propelling him to the top of the Hollywood game in the 1970s. Then tragedy struck. During an equestrian competition, his horse threw him and he landed on his neck. His injury was so severe that he was paralyzed from the neck down. But Reeve had a vision that would guide him through the next 10 years. At his forty-third birthday party he announced that he would stand up and make a toast at his fiftieth.

This vision propelled him across the globe, making countless speeches and pleads for money for spinal cord research. He was dedicated to finding a cure. Unfortunately, this vision did not come to fruition, and he did not stand to toast his friends on any birthday following the accident. Sadder was his death, at the age of 52, of a heart attack. His memory and his vision, however, still guide his foundation to find a cure in the future.

In his book *The Power of Purpose*, Dick Leider interviewed hundreds of people in their seventies and eighties. He asked them two simple questions: "If you could live your life over again, what would you change?" and "What is the wisdom that you would pass on?"

One of the most frequent answers given was that they would have had a better vision for their life's direction and that this vision would have made a difference.

Those answers from our elders send a clear-cut message: Find a vision for your life that has meaning. According to the ancient philosopher Seneca, "When a man does not know what harbor he is sailing for, no wind is the right wind." Zig Ziglar, a present-day motivational guru, has noted that the happiest people he knows are those who are working toward a vision, whereas the most bored and miserable people are drifting along with no worthwhile objectives in mind. They sail with any wind.

The issue with vision is twofold. First, many people do not know their true vision, and second, their career choices are not in line with their true vision. Becoming aware of your true vision and having that vision aligned with your career may be the most difficult task a person can accomplish, but it is essential. The following drills will help.

DON'T WAIT FOR YOUR MORTALITY SANDWICH

Deborah Winger called it "a mortality sandwich." When she was young, she had planned to be a researcher for criminal investigations. As Winger describes it, she wanted to be an investigator just like in the show *CSI*. Then she had a terrible but fortuitous, and almost too close of an encounter with a truck. It was this crash that gave her a clear look at her mortality. This event inspired her to change direction and follow her true vision—to be an actress. And as we know, she has had an incredible career, starring in such mega-hits as *An Officer and a Gentleman, Urban Cowboy,* and *Terms of Endearment.*

Don't wait for your mortality sandwich. Eat life up!

ALIGNING YOUR CAREER WITH YOUR VISION

Finding a better direction was easy for John Sculley. When Steve Jobs was looking for a man to hold the helm and steer his new company, Apple Computer, he approached Sculley. At the time, Sculley was president of Pepsico and was having a wonderful career. However, when Steve Jobs approached him and asked him if he wanted to make sugar water all his life or help change the world, the choice was easy for Sculley. He wanted to make a meaningful difference, so he left and joined Apple so that he could help change the world.

Are you struggling to align your career with your vision? The first step is to create a purpose statement. A purpose statement is a vision about what we believe will give meaning to our life.

Here are a few questions to guide you in developing an effective purpose statement.

- Who do you admire and why?
- What have been some of the greatest contributions to our world?
- What do you see as meaningful?
- What significant contributions would you like to make to the world?

The next step is to list your values. Martin Luther King Jr. once stated, "I do not want to have the finer things in life.

All I want to leave behind is a committed life. King valued a committed life, a life dedicated to changing human rights.

What do you value most? These may include money, civil rights, creating a useful product, helping the homeless, or other values such as creating a better world or a better environment for our children. List 10 of your key values.

Now here is the kicker. Pick two or three careers (or different jobs within your current career path) that you think are in line with your true vision. Write a persuasive paragraph for each career, as if you were writing to a friend, and tell this friend how your purpose statement and values are aligned with this particular career.

The paragraphs that are difficult to write, that is, the careers that had to be bent and pushed to fit into your statement and values, are probably not a good choice. This career choice is out of sync with your true vision. On the other hand, the paragraph that was the easiest to write, the one that was the best fit for your purpose and values, will be the correct choice and a step toward following your vision.

Henry David Thoreau once stated, "In the long run, men hit only what they aim at." I would add "We need to know where to aim." This chapter will point you in the right direction.

CHAPTER THREE

Race into the Strength Zone

Miguel Cervantes once wrote that the man who is prepared has his battle half fought. Individuals who develop a plan are destined to be prepared for what lies ahead. More important, when the plan incorporates our strengths, we are preparing for our success. When Lance Armstrong developed a plan that involved using his strengths, he laid the foundation for his destiny as the greatest cyclist the world has ever seen.

In his early years, Lance did not have a precise racing plan. He would win short races with a "go all-out aggressive, in-your-face" attitude. His strength was to use his explosive power for most of the race. Lance knew, however, that this style would never get him to the top of the racing world and win the long haul of the Tour de France.

Lance developed a plan that enabled him to use his strengths—to use his explosive power at the correct moments of the race. Every racer is given a Tour bible, a guidebook that shows every stage of the course with profiles of the route. With this guide, Lance created a plan that allowed him to stay close to the leaders, but also permitted him to explode with power when needed. His plan maximized his strengths and led him to victory a record seven times in a row at the Tour de France.

While Clarence Quillen never raced in the Tour de France, he used the same principle of maximizing his strengths to find his road to success in the homebuilding world. But Clarence was not always in this industry. In fact, he started his career as an engineer at NASA. He lost his job, however, during a round of downsizing in the 1970s.

Clarence was never one to wallow in self-pity. So, the day after his layoff, he went to Castaic Lake and sat by the shore. He wrote down three main aspects to guide him on his next vocational journey. He first created a list of his top strengths. Some of those strengths included being creative, having integrity, thinking critically, possessing a love for learning, and working very hard. Then he created a list of his "work wants," such as he wanted to be independent and work for himself as well as create something he could leave behind. Last, he created a list of his true friends, those he could rely on in times of trouble.

Quillen sat on the shore for two days working on his three key lists. When he felt the lists were complete, he analyzed what they meant for his future. Clarence decided that they led him into the construction business. Emphasizing his key strengths placed him on a path that today is a multimillion-dollar homebuilding business in Los Angeles.

Today, many business experts purport the same philosophy about being in our strength zone at work. One expert, Marcus Buckingham, has popularized this notion in his best-selling business book, *First, Break all the Rules*. Buckingham touts that our productivity and happiness are a function of how well we use our strengths. The following drills demonstrate how to implement your strengths.

MAKE THE INVISIBLE VISIBLE

Mark Legatte owned the public relations company Sincerely Real. One of his primary tasks was to question CEOs and heads of staff at companies and strip down their message to the bare minimum. His tactics made him highly successful because he was always able to fulfill the needs of his clients.

Then Mark got bored at his job and he wanted to move on in his life and career. But Mark did not know where to go or what to do. He also did not really know why he had been so successful in the past. He enlisted the help of an executive coach, who, Mark said, helped to make the invisible visible.

His coach enlightened Mark about his true strengths. From their discussions, Mark discovered that he was very empathetic and knew the right questions to ask at the right time. Based on his discussions with his coach, Mark realized that he too should become an executive coach. Today, he has a thriving coaching business called Essentially Real.

The first step to developing an effective plan for life is to make the invisible visible. You must first take a hard look inward and ask yourself what signature strengths have contributed to your success.

List your five signature strengths:

1. _____

2. _____

3. _____

4. _____

5. _____

BE HAPPIER

Martin Seligman, a professor of psychology at Penn State University, has discovered that individuals who use their signature strengths in their careers will not only be more successful but also be much happier.

How often do you use your strengths? Do you think you use them more than 20 percent of the time at work? 50 percent of the time? 75 percent of the time?

To discover this percentage, first look at your signature strength list. Next, record each time you use that strength during a given day for the week. Do this in two-hour increments over an eight-hour workday. For instance, if two of your key strengths are creativity and being a good listener, and you use those strengths each once during the day (that is, any time during a two-hour period), then you have a percentage of 50 percent (two times two hours for an eight-hour period).

If you discover that you are using strengths for less than an average of 20 percent on any given day during the week, you may need a change to get back on track. Ask yourself these two questions: In what areas of work might I use my strengths more often? And, can I take on different projects to use more of my strengths?

Develop strategies to implement your strengths and you will be much happier when observing your increase in success.

STRENGTH ATTRACTION

Do you want to attract more clients? Then use your strengths to your advantage.

New Age books, such as *The Secret*, speak to the Law of Attraction. In short, this law is about Karma: What you give, you will receive. What you put out into your world, you will attract. If you give off positive energy, positive events will come your way. If you give off negative thoughts, you will attract unwanted events.

You may or may not believe in the Law of Attraction. But every sales professional and business needs to continually attract new clients to stay afloat.

One simple method to attract new clients is to use your talents. When you are engaging in your strengths, you are giving off great confidence, great joy, and great positive energy. When this happens, people will gravitate toward you. By following the principles of the Law of Attraction, you will get more clients by giving away great energy.

Are you using your unique strengths to gain new clients?

Perhaps you are a great chef. Have you done any cooking events to attract new clients? People will be interested in you because you are giving off great energy when you are cooking. It is not about the cooking, it is about the positive heat you will give during the event.

Perhaps you are a superb artist, or simply love to paint. Are you teaching any art classes in the hope of gaining new clients? When you are involved in painting, you will be colorful and your energy will be magnetic.

To attract more prospects, look at the list of your five signature strengths. Now, ask yourself if you are using these strengths to your advantage. If not, create a plan to incorporate one of these unused strengths each week as a vehicle to gain more business.

COMBINE YOUR STRENGTHS

If you combine your strengths, you double your advantage. It worked for Mark McCormack, who started IMG (International Management Group) as well as the sports agency business.

Mark McCormack was a great negotiator as well as quite a golf enthusiast. As a young lawyer, he befriended Arnold Palmer and persuaded him to allow McCormack to manage his everyday activities and finances outside the golf course. That way, Arnold could focus all his energies on golf. With only a handshake, Mark became Arnold's agent, and the sports agent industry had begun. While Mark would have been a very successful lawyer, when he combined his strengths, he had success beyond measure.

To double your advantage, look at your signature strength list. Can you combine any of those strengths? Perhaps you are a great speaker and a great golfer. Can you begin leading seminars with clients about how golf mirrors life? Create a plan using a combination of your strengths and you will double your competitive advantage.

CHAPTER FOUR

Set Your Flame

At the 2000 Olympic games in Sydney, Australia, Kathy Freeman became of symbol of reconciliation for a country. Although of Aboriginal descent, Kathy saw herself as no different from any other Australian athlete who was representing her country. But she was much more—Kathy was uniting a country to look beyond race and to help overcome the difficulties of the past.

As a runner, Kathy is propelled by the moment and has mentioned that she wins her races when she masters her emotions. On the flip side, Kathy has discovered that she loses races when she becomes too aggressive at the start. If she starts too quickly, she will peak too early and burn out by the end of the race, losing in the last 100 meters.

But on this day in Australia, she controlled her internal flame, running a beautiful 400-meter race with an amazing kick in the last 50 meters to win the Olympic gold. As she ran around the track in her victory lap, she held both of the flags of her county, the Aboriginal and the Australian, something she always dreamed she would do in front of her country.

Great performers know their internal flame. They know at what level it has to be set so they can perform at their best. The internal flame is also known as one's intensity level. A useful analogy is the flame on the stove when you are heating soup. When the flame is set too low, the soup will take a long time to warm up. If the flame is set too high, the soup will come to a boil too quickly and perhaps burn or spill over the sides. To heat the soup most effectively, you need to set the flame at the appropriate level.

To be able to cook in business, you need to be able to adjust your flame to the correct living temperature. Sometimes you may need to turn up the heat and at other times lower it. The following drills will help you set your internal flame.

KNOW YOUR FLAME SETTING

Kobe Bryant, one of the greatest basketball players of his generation, has mentioned that he tries to keep his flame set in the middle, not too high and not too low. This allows him to keep his emotions under control and to play his best basketball under extreme pressure.

The first step to discovering your most effective internal flame setting is through awareness. To accomplish this step, first recall an event in which you performed brilliantly, a perfect close or a great presentation during an important meeting. Next, rank your intensity level, from 0 to 100 in 10-point increments, with 0 being totally flat and 100 being too high. For instance, 20 could represent "somewhat flat," 50 being "somewhat energized," with the score of 80 being "very energized." You may find that you perform your best with an intensity level of 40, while Kobe Bryant is best at a setting of 60.

Repeat the procedure, but this time, recall an event in which you totally choked, such as an error-filled close or presentation. Rank your intensity level. You may find that you were at a 90. Everyone is different, however. Someone in your office may find that she performs her best at 80 and her worst when her intensity is set at 20.

This awareness experience allows you to gain a better understanding of what level to set your flame under pressure.

GET COOKING WITH YOUR BLUE BIKE

If you are a slow starter, then perhaps your flame is set too low. Indications of a low intensity level include feelings of not being ready, not being warmed up enough, and a feeling of not being with it. Being a slow starter can lead to a variety of problems, such as a loss of focus and making too many errors at the start of your presentation or negotiation.

If you are a notoriously slow starter, then get a mental tool to get you pumped up quickly. It could be an image or a story from your past. Muhammad Ali used such a story to find the right intensity in the ring.

As a young boy, he loved his blue bike. One day, he parked it in front of the grocery store only to find when he came out that someone had clipped the lock and rode off with his prized possession. He never found the bike again or who had stolen it. But Ali used this story to his advantage. Every time he entered the ring, he would point at his opponent and say, "You're the guy who stole my blue bike." That got him fired up in a hurry.

Do you have a story or image such as Ali's which could get the juices flowing quickly? If so, punch up that image and use it to your advantage.

BE CAREFUL WITH ANGER

Athletes sometimes use anger to kick-start a bad outing or to remedy a slide in performance. John McEnroe, the Hall of Fame tennis player, was notorious for this process. When things on the court were not going as planned and usually when he was losing, he would throw his famous fits, screaming at ball boys or his favorite target, chair umpires.

These tirades were part of McEnroe's arsenal. These emotional outbursts were a method for John to help elevate his intensity level and channel his focus. They were also a mechanism to throw off an opponent's mental game. Sometimes, John would go on a tirade for five minutes, icing an opponent. John won many matches by throwing a fit and swinging the momentum in his favor. McEnroe mastered the ability to harness anger into victory.

You too may feel like you can perform better when you get a bit of the angry verve. What is actually happening is that the anger is getting you pumped up and increasing your intensity level.

You must be cautioned, however, against using anger to your advantage. Phil Jackson, head coach of the Chicago Bulls and the Los Angeles Lakers, mentioned that while you need a warrior attitude, you must not lose control and erupt. Phil is referring to our inability to act rational when we get too mad. Scientists have indicated that anger is based in the primitive part of the brain and is a carryover from our prehistoric years. Getting angry quickly and losing our temper helped us to stay alive in a hostile world. Excessive anger, however, can make us lose our focus and our ability to remain rational under the heat of pressure situations.

Winston Churchill once said to a impatient general in a fit of rage during a heated discussion, "You do not possess your emotions—they possess you!" Tirades worked for McEnroe, but they may not work for you. They will probably possess you to say and do something you do not want. Most likely, it is best to find other tools besides anger to get you pumped and inspired for the moment at hand.

GO SLOW TO TURN DOWN THE FLAME

Sometimes, the flame can get out of hand, creating havoc with a negotiation or sales pitch and it may be due to nerves. When we are nervous, our body surges with hormones such as epinephrine and adrenaline. These hormones can act as stimulants and create a surge in our internal flame.

Gary Player developed a unique mental strategy for dealing with the pressures of competitive golf. For many golfers under pressure, their swing speed gets too quick, which can ruin the best of swings. To remedy this difficulty, Gary does everything at a slower pace before a tournament. He takes his clubs out of his car more slowly than usual, he meanders to the tee, and he even ties his shoes unhurriedly before a tournament round. The slowness of action allows Gary's swing to stay in rhythm and pace.

Try the Gary Player technique to help turn down your flame. Slow down a bit when you feel the nerves creeping into a situation. Be more deliberate than usual with each word or action. This should counterbalance your nerves and keep your flame at the right level.

TRY EASY

Our flame can be set too high when we try too hard. We have all heard the old success adage "Just give 110 percent." Giving all you have, however, may actually be detrimental to performance. Trying too hard can negatively affect high achievement.

In a test with Olympic runners, coaches in the first race asked their athletes to give 100 percent. In the second race, though, the coaches asked their runners to turn it down a notch, to try easy at about 85 percent. To their amazement, the second race times were faster than the first. Trying too hard increased the pressure, which decreased their ability to speed down the track.

Instead of trying too hard, you may want to try easy. This feeling is best described by Olympic skater Scott Hamilton as "a refined indifference." He skated his best when he did not force any movements, but rather just let them happen. Trying easy is being actively engaged in the moment, but not forcing a great performance, close, or sales pitch—just letting it happen.

CHAPTER FIVE

Get a Charge from Risk

Theodore Roosevelt acknowledged his penchant for risk-taking when he spoke before the Hamilton Club in Chicago in 1899 and told his audience, "Far better it is to dare mighty things, to win glorious triumphs, even though checkered by failure, than to take rank with those poor spirits who neither enjoy much nor suffer much, because they live in the gray twilight that knows not victory nor defeat." From history, we have read that Teddy led the charge up the famous San Juan Hill with his Rough Riders in the Spanish-American War. President Roosevelt was also a trust buster, going against the big-time capitalism of his day. Teddy loved a good fight that had lots of risk—this is what motivated his charge through life.

Another person who gets a charge out of risk is the golfer Phil Mickelson. Take this poignant but tragic story of his high-risk way of playing: The scene was the 2006 U.S. Open. Phil had a one-stroke lead standing on the tee box on the seventy-second hole. All he needed was a par to capture his first U.S. Open championship. Most players might play it safe and use a utility wood or iron to hit the fairway—but not Phil. He took out his driver and sliced it far left (he is a lefty), almost hitting it out of bounds. From that point, he tried to hit his next shot around the tree that lay directly in front of him and the green. Phil hit the tree and his ball dropped straight down. He then smashed an iron out of the rough, which landed in the greenside bunker. He blasted out over the green, flipped his next shot to two feet, and sunk the putt for a double bogey. He lost the championship by just one stroke, to Geoff Olgivy.

Phil's fans, and he has millions of them, were all cringing from the experience.

Why didn't he just play it safe and go for a par? All he needed was a par. Why did he make such a poor decision?

The answer is simple. Phil Mickelson is an extreme risk taker. This style of play is what energizes him. In fact, Phil is no different from a sky diver, race car driver, or bungee jumper. High-risk takers become bored very easily, so they seek out activities that are exciting. They not only thrive on the rush, they need the rush.

This need may be due to their neurological makeup. Psychologists have recently shown that high-risk personality styles have low serotonin in the brain. Serotonin is a neurotransmitter that helps the brain function. Having low serotonin is analogous to a car idling in low gear. High-risk behavior stimulates the serotonin production in the brain of high-risk takers and shifts their brain into high gear. The stimulation of high-risk situations, therefore, is rewarding and these individuals gravitate toward this type of behavior. For Phil, he gets a rush by playing for broke on most of his shots.

Phil Mickelson exemplifies the old axiom "Live by the sword and die by the sword." His go-for-broke style has made him one of the best and most well-loved golfers of his generation, yet it has also ruined a few tournament rounds—and the final round of the 2006 U.S. Open was no exception.

Many believe taking risks and exhibiting this style is essential for success. Former IBM chairman John Akers says, "The people who are playing it totally safe are never going to have either the fun or the reward of the people who decide to take some risks." According to Akers, "There is an incredible excitement to risk taking. There is an increase in energy. The adrenaline flows and the awareness is heightened. You have a greater sense of aliveness. Life assumes a richer hue." These statements are clearly spoken by a man who loves to take risks in his life.

Marc Cuban exhibits that hue in life from which John Akers speaks. Mark Cuban is a well-known and flamboyant self-made billionaire. He rose to riches by co-founding MicroSolutions, which he sold to Compuserve in 1990. He then co-founded broadcast.com, an Internet sports radio broadcasting service, which he sold to Yahoo in 1999 for $5.9 billion, at the peak of the dotcom bubble. He also loves his sports and is currently the owner of the Dallas Mavericks basketball team.

Cuban's philosophy for business is to take risks to gain something, and according to him, "If you do not have the courage to get out of your comfort zone, you will never be successful." Cuban believes that risk and success go hand in hand.

Marc Cuban, John Akers, Phil Mickelson, and Theodore Roosevelt have the quality of being a risk taker in common. Their life takes on a glow when risk is involved. Without it, their life would be dull. Thus, we could extrapolate that these individuals became successful because they intuitively brought risk into their lives. Risk helped them achieve their greatness, regardless of venue.

RISK AWARENESS

Are you a risk taker? Do you have a risk-taking personality? Psychologists have labeled this a *T* personality type.

Here are a few questions to assess whether or not you are a risk taker.

1. Do you like driving fast in the rain?
2. Do you enjoy a good roller coaster?
3. Do you like downhill skiing when there is a chance of injury?
4. Do you enjoy living life on the edge?
5. Are your decisions considered risky and edgy?

If you answered yes to four out of five of these questions, you probably have a risk-taking personality.

More important, are you using this personality style to your advantage?

Or, have you lost the glow in your life? Perhaps by adding some risk, you can change the hue of your world.

GET RISKY WITH A PLAN

While risk taking may be essential to some to fill that void or boost their adrenaline, don't believe it is always done without a purpose. It is rarely done haphazardly by anyone, either in sports or business.

Consider Paul Neal "Red" Adair, who became famous for his expertise in the extinguishing of oil well fires. Through his work, he built a reputation as the best oil well firefighter in the world. In 1991, his company put out the Gulf War oil fires and received a special letter of recognition from President George H. W. Bush for the work, which was completed in just nine months.

You might figure that a man who faced the heat of death every day at work would have a plan. He did. Red said that fighting a fire is like going into battle and mounting an invasion. You start with a battle plan, gather your men and equipment, and then attack.

If you are like Teddy Roosevelt, Phil Mickelson, or Marc Cuban, be risky but have a plan. Engaging in high-risk behavior doesn't mean that you act impulsively. Just because you may not want a net when you leap does not mean you do not have a plan when you land.

CHAPTER SIX

Find Your Flow

Charlie Nickell was asked to present his sales strategies at the next national Mona Vie convention. Mona Vie is a network marketing company that sells a fruit drink, containing 19 different fruits, with the most popular being the acai berry. Charlie had entered the company nine months before and had become its top salesman on the West Coast. The leadership was so impressed with his rapid rise and network marketing skills that they wanted him to share it with others in the corporation.

Charlie had reservations about accepting such a grand invitation. He had never spoken before more than 20 people, let alone two thousand of his colleagues. But he agreed. On the day of his presentation, Charlie was all nerves, but as he walked to the podium, he felt calm and peaceful. As he gave his speech, he was brimming with enthusiasm. It seemed to him that everyone in the audience was hanging on his every word. Every humorous comment produced a huge laugh. Every word spoken came crisply from his lips. While the presentation lasted 60 minutes, it seemed but seconds. Charlie felt a sense of great joy and honor and wanted the presentation to never end.

Charlie was in the Zone. The Zone is that magical place where everything feels right, you can do no wrong, and the difficult seems easy. It is a place we long to be but rarely find.

One of the first psychologists to study the Zone was Mihaly Csikzentmihalyi. Instead of calling it the Zone, he calls it *flow*, and has found that everyone can experience flow, from athletes to musicians to business professionals. After recording the responses of hundreds of subjects, Dr. Csikzentmihalyi discovered that certain conditions have to be present to reach this optimal state. These include such factors as a challenging situation, an optimal intensity level, complete focus on the task, a feeling of supreme confidence, and feelings of joy.

Although there are certain conditions that help to produce the Zone, everyone describes this place a bit differently. The Hall of Fame golfer Sam Snead described the Zone as a *cool mad*—he is intense but relaxed. Bobby Locke, another supreme golfer, said he found the Zone when he possessed a calm deportment. The author Timothy Hallinan has commented that his most creative experiences come when he is writing hot. He doesn't analyze anything; he just takes off with his thoughts. I have found that my best writing comes to me when I start off slow, critiquing my work before moving into new material.

Given that the flow state is unique to the individual, we need to create our own road map to finding the Zone more often. This starts with awareness. The following drills guide you toward increasing the probability of finding the Zone.

KNOW THYSELF

Pick three different events where you felt you were in the Zone. They can be from a variety of venues, from sports to music to business, or from the same situation (for example, speaking to groups). The characteristics for the Zone should be the same for you across different situations. Now address these questions for each event:

> Was there anything unique that happened before this event? (For example, did you overly prepare, or not prepare?)
>
> What were your feelings during the event? (For example, were you excited? nervous? calm? energized?)
>
> What were you thinking during the event? (For example, were you confident, or unsure?)
>
> Were there any special circumstances during the event? (For example, smaller audience? Bigger audience? No audience?)

To find out how we get into the Zone, we also need to know why we perform at our worst, or choke under pressure. Do the same as before, but pick three different events where you performed terribly. Address the following questions:

> Was there anything unique that happened before this event?
>
> What were your feelings during the event?
>
> What were you thinking during the event?
>
> Were there any special circumstances during the event?

Now look at the two composite sketches—one when you performed brilliantly and one when you performed terribly. What are the key differences? List three of those differences.

1. _____

2. _____

3. _____

"Know thyself" was an imperative according to William Shakespeare. It is an imperative to taking the best path to achieve at the highest level.

CHAPTER SEVEN

Stick with the Basics

Thomas Friedman was blessed to have a teacher like Hattie Steinberg. In fact, Hattie was the only journalism teacher of this three-time Pulitzer Prize winning–*New York Times* columnist and best-selling author.

Friedman said that his success has been based on sticking with the basics, and Hattie pounded this principle into his head every day in high school. Those fundamentals included how to accurately transcribe a quote, how to write a lead, how to always act in a professional way, and to always stick to your guns about a story.

In one such instance, Friedman interviewed an ad exec for the high school paper who used a four-letter word. He was unsure whether or not to run the story with the profanity, but Hattie said to print it. The ad man almost lost his job when it appeared, but Thomas learned that sticking with the basics leads to first-class journalism, and he consistently follows this principle in his columns and books.

Sticking with the basics can also lead to world-class hitting. Tony Gwynn is considered one of the purest hitters of his generation. He captured eight batting titles and has a lifetime batting average of .338, one of the highest of all time. When Tony's game took a dive, he would simply go back to the fundamentals. To accomplish this, he would hit a Wiffle ball on a tee. Tony believed that the sound and the spin of the Wiffle ball gave him all the information he needed to get back on track. If he hit the Wiffle ball correctly, there would be a whooshing sound as it flew through the air instead of a whinier, spinning sound. If he hit the ball underneath, the ball would have an excessive backspin, and if he hit it too much on the top, it would have a topspin. Furthermore, Tony knew that if his hands were too quick to the inside, the ball would have an inside-out spin. If his hands were too late, the spin would be outside-to-in.

If two of the greatest in their respective fields believe that sticking to the basics led to their success, then such a strategy should work in any field, including business. Unfortunately, many individuals neglect or just forget the basics when they believe they have mastered a skill.

MAKE A BASIC LIST

John Wooden would start with the basics of all basics. On the first day of the season, Wooden would share one of his greatest pearls of wisdom and say, "Today we are going to learn how to put on our socks and shoes just so." To Wooden, any wrinkle in the sock would cause rubbing and could cause a blister. Blisters keep you from practicing, which keeps you from getting better.

One easy way to reinstate the basics in your performance is by making a mental checklist of key fundamentals. Orel Hershiser, an all-time great pitcher for the Dodgers, did just that. Even after 30 years of playing baseball, Orel Hershiser would write down a list of basic pitching principles and then go over this list before each game. His list included such basics as:

Keep a good posture on the mound

Good weight distribution on my feet

Proper length of my step back

Have an aggressive leg kick

Focus my eyes

Have a good follow through

What do you believe are the basics for being a great manager? A great salesperson? A great accountant? A great negotiator? Do you have a basic list for your profession?

If not, now is the time to make that list of the essentials. Post it on your computer or where you will see it often. Then follow those basics before each interaction. While your list may not include a Wiffle ball and tee, your items will make a hit toward your success.

KEEP IT SIMPLE

Tony Dungy, the former head coach of the NFL's Indianapolis Colts, learned a key from his mentor, Chuck Noll, a former head coach of the Pittsburgh Steelers: When you're not successful, or you're struggling or having problems, do less, not more. According to Dungy, when the Steelers were not playing well, Coach Noll looked to cut back, to simplify, to get back to the basics.

Do you try to do more when times get tough? Are your strategies getting more complicated as sales go down?

Perhaps the easiest and best solution is to scale back—to simplify and focus back on the fundamentals. It has worked for two of the most successful coaches in NFL history.

CHAPTER EIGHT

Through the Uprights

Tom Dempsey was born with a partial right arm, and only half a right foot. To most, that would have ruled out a life in football, but Tom had a different belief system.

He developed a customized kicking shoe that fit his disfigured foot, with a flat toe about three inches in diameter. With hard work, Tom mastered the technique of his special equipment. He would swing his leg and drive the ball like a polo player using a mallet, propelling a football long distances.

Unbelievably, Tom made it to the NFL and landed a job as kicker for a new team, the New Orleans Saints. The Saints were finishing up a dismal season. With only one win to date, they were playing a much better team, the Detroit Lions. With just two seconds remaining on the clock, Tom Dempsey had a chance to kick the game-winning field goal. But there was much more than just the game on the line: history was at stake. Dempsey hit a 63-yard field goal through the uprights—the longest field goal ever, propelling the Saints to a 19–17 victory. That kick was a defining moment in his life. Using his special strength,

Dempsey became an inspiration to millions on that day in 1970.

All true winners have learned to turn an apparent weakness into a strength. David Meador is a champion in his own right, winning the U.S. blind golf championship. But that is not what makes him special. David has learned to turn his blindness into a platform for his professional speaking business. David speaks around the country about focus—yes, focus. He shares with his audiences that blindness has allowed him to remain focused on the important aspects of life. His blindness does not allow him to be distracted by television, YouTube, or text messaging, aspects of everyday life that can deter many of us from achieving our potential. As David puts it, he is the only guy in America who can walk into Home Depot and not be distracted by anything on the shelves.

David's blindness is his strength. In fact, his message is so powerful that he usually receives a standing ovation. David's apparent weakness is his most poignant ally.

Voltaire likened life to a game of cards. Each player must accept the cards dealt to him. But once those cards are in hand, he alone decides how to play them to win the game. Tom Dempsey and David Meador took their cards and played a great hand. What cards have you been dealt?

PLAYING YOUR CARDS

Most people run away from their weaknesses, or just deny their existence. Sometimes, it is too painful to acknowledge them or just too energy draining to work on them in our fast-paced lifestyle. What we don't realize is that many of our weaknesses can become great strengths. It all depends on our perspective.

President Andrew Jackson turned the apparent weakness of having an excessively hot temper into a negotiating strength. Jackson's hot temper did cause him much trouble—he carried two bullets in his body from duels and gun fights. He even once threatened to kill his own vice president. But he used his hot temper to his advantage during a banking crisis in his presidency. A group of bankers came to him asking for a bailout from the government. He thought their pleas were unjustified and acted out with such fury that they disregarded their proposal. Once they left, his fury subsided and so did the issue.

Perhaps you can use your fiery temper as an occasional negotiating tool.

On the opposite side of the emotional spectrum, perhaps you are a bit timid and unassertive. Many may see those traits as weaknesses in the world of selling. But it is a matter of perspective. Being timid and unassertive can greatly act to your advantage, if you let it. Those traits can be seen as the soft-sell approach. Many individuals would prefer to buy from someone who is less assertive than overly domineering.

List five of your apparent weaknesses. For each, describe how they can be turned into your advantage.

1. _____
   How to use it as an advantage:_____
   _____

2. _____
   How to use it as an advantage:_____
   _____

3. _____
   How to use it as an advantage:_____
   _____

4. _____
   How to use it as an advantage:_____
   _____

5. _____
   How to use it as an advantage:_____
   _____

CHAPTER NINE

Start with a Beginner's Mind

In 1992, John Daly was the ninth alternate to get into the last major of the year, the PGA championships. He was at home in Memphis, not playing much or practicing his golf. That week, he was not expecting to play, but by Wednesday night he discovered that he had become the first alternate. The problem was that the tournament site was 15 hours away, at Crooked Stick in Indianapolis, Indiana. John went for it and drove all night to get there, in case he got the call.

As fate would have it, John Daly made it into the tournament. He walked to the first tee on Thursday morning, however, without having the opportunity to play a practice round on one of the longest and toughest courses in PGA major history. On his first round, John shot a 69, placing him two strokes ahead of the field. The second day he shot a 67, and again had the lead. He finished off Saturday and Sunday with a 3-stroke victory.

Most pros will play a few practice rounds before a tournament to develop a battle plan. But this process can be a double-edged sword. With a practice round, you develop expectations about how you will play. At times, this can be constructive, but it also can be destructive if your play is poor.

Without a practice round, John did not have the negative baggage of any bad shots. He came to the tournament with a blank slate, a tabula rasa. He had no preconceived notions from any history. Daly just gripped it and ripped it and the rest was history.

Coming to the table with no expectations can, at times, help your sales performance. It did for Craig Patrick. He had owned a pizza parlor in Mammoth Lakes, California, but sold it to move his family to Los Angeles. He no longer wanted to own a pizza business, and ended up selling Land Rovers in the South Bay. Within just a few months, he became the number one salesman, without any automotive sales experience. As he describes it, "I treated everyone the same. I came to the table without any prejudices or biases from the past. I treated everyone like a world-class prospect." Those high expectations led to Craig's success.

In many cases in a business setting, especially in a sales setting, we come to the table with expectations, some high and some low. Rarely do we come without expectations—with a tabula rasa. Unfortunately, having low preconceptions of prospects and clients can create a ceiling of limitations because they create biases in our behaviors and interactions. This phenomenon has been called the self-fulfilling prophecy. Put simply, our expectations will influence our interactions and, in turn, those interactions can become self-fulfilling.

In the famous self-fulfilling prophecy study conducted with children in the 1960s, students were randomly selected to various classrooms. One group of students was labeled "intellectual bloomers," when in fact they were no different from the other students. The teachers, however, treated these particular students differently because they believed the students were advanced. They gave these students more positive feedback and engaging communication. The other "normal" students received less preferential treatment from the teachers. The intellectual bloomers, in turn, had better academic scores at the end of the school year than the other student groups. The teachers' expectations were self-fulfilled.

This same phenomenon can apply to Craig Patrick or any other salesperson. If Craig had negative expectations for certain clients, his sales would have dropped at Land Rover. That is, if he believed some prospects were less likely to purchase a Land Rover than other prospects (for example, because of how they dress, or their race), his interactions would have changed. With such expectations, he may treat some prospects worse than others from the beginning. He may rush his answers and be less engaged in conversation. He may seem distracted and not interested in them. In turn, Craig would connect less. His lower expectations would be fulfilled with decreased sales.

BEING AWARE OF YOUR BIASES

The first step in reducing the self-fulfilling prophecy is to be aware of your biases and expectations.

Do you come to the table with certain biases? If so, ask if they have ever hurt your performance in the past? If the answer is yes, then change your expectations.

Becoming aware of your expectations is the first step to changing them in a positive direction.

HAVE THE HIGHEST EXPECTATIONS FOR EVERYONE

Be like Craig Patrick. Come to the table with the highest expectations for every client. See every client as wonderful and a great prospect.

How do you act when you know a prospect has a high probability of buying the product? Are you more jovial? Are you more engaging?

Treat every client with the highest level of expectations and watch your pocketbook be fulfilled because of your great results.

PART 2

EMOTIONAL PREPAREDNESS

Champions are ready for any event. Winners like Rudy Giuliani have developed plans for catastrophes so that they can respond effectively. Winners such as Willie Mays and Joe Montana have chosen to respond to life with an optimistic outlook, regardless of outcome. Champions use past experiences, both failures and successes, as bricks to build their confidence.

This section illustrates how to be emotionally prepared for the worst, but be optimistic for the best.

CHAPTER TEN

Plan for the Best, but Prepare for the Worst

Rudy Giuliani is known as "America's Mayor." He gained fame as the mayor of New York City during the horrific shock of September 11, 2001. When this terrible situation happened, Rudy Giuliani looked like a man who could handle the pressure: He did not panic.

Why? Was it his personality? Was it his upbringing?

Giuliani followed the lead of another great politician, George Washington, who said, "If we are wise, let us prepare for the worst." Giuliani has said that New York City has a crisis every month. As such, he and his staff created plans for responding to every difficulty they could imagine for their city. According to Giuliani, he had a plan to deal with weather catastrophes as well as biological warfare. He had a plan for everything—or so he thought—until September 11, 2001. Giuliani and his staff had never foreseen a plane deliberately crashing into a building (or worse, to be used as a missile to destroy the World Trade Center).

According to Giuliani, however, he was ready for the worst because he had all those other crisis plans in place. While none were the exact plan for this terrorist attack, they allowed Rudy and his staff to translate those actions into effective responses for a horrific and unforeseen crisis. As a result of his preparation, Rudy Giuliani took on fame as a leader that still shines today.

While nothing in sports could compare to the horrific tragedy of the New York and Pentagon terrorist attacks, athletes must deal with their own personal adversities and crises that can occur during a competition. The most successful ones are ready for anything that may happen because they have prepared for adversity. Al Orter became the greatest shot-putter of all time because he prepared for failure.

While Al Orter had arms of steel and a body built for power, he benefited greatly from his mental preparation. He knew champions had to overcome continual adversity. Therefore, he would be ready to perform under adverse conditions. Orter would imagine the day of the Olympic finals, in the pouring rain. He would visualize the throwing area in atrociously slippery conditions, yet he would still throw with great technique. Or, sometimes, he would picture in his mind that he had one more throw attempt in the Olympic finals, with the Russians trailing just behind him. He had performed poorly in his previous throws, but his mental rehearsal envisioned him responding to that adversity with a new world record on his last attempt. His training regimen helped him control his emotions under adversity and win gold medals in four consecutive Olympiads, from 1956 to 1968.

In any endeavor, events rarely go as planned. Spontaneous and difficult questions can arise during key meetings. Your boss may change the deadline for the proposal from one week to two days. Your plane gets canceled, so you miss your important meeting, and so on and so on and so on.

Unfortunately, most people follow a Pollyannaish approach rather than a Giulianiesque one. They believe that only good events will happen to them. Furthermore, they do not want to open their mind or spirit to all the bad events that can occur because they believe it to be bad luck. Unfortunately, with such an attitude, when the worst does come, they are not ready. They may freeze up or simply recoil from the adversity, which becomes their downfall.

Pat Riley, the championship-winning NBA coach, said there comes a moment that defines winners and losers. The true warrior understands and seizes the moment. Riley said, "Know this: You will experience one of those defining moments. And it will define you as an achiever. Prepare for that moment and know that it's coming, and you increase your chances for winning your way through it."

Failure is not about the adversity itself, but rather how we respond to the adversity. Failure is having a failed or ineffective response to a difficult situation. Success, on the other hand, is responding positively and effectively to a difficult situation. Those who have a planned positive response will become a success. The following will help you prepare for the best but plan for the worst.

DEVELOP AN ADVERSITY PLAN

To be a winner, develop an adversity plan. First write down a list of five relevant events that could happen during the week or month that could be considered an obstacle or hurdle. Next, create a corresponding list of positive responses to the adversity. Remember, it is not the event that defines you as a person, but rather your response will determine whether or not you can overcome it and grow from it.

Adversity	**Positive Response**
1.	
2.	
3.	
4.	
5.	

PREPARATION IMPLIES PERSPIRATION

Creating an adversity plan is only the first step. Implementing the plan is the next step. Implementation can occur with visualizations such as Al Orter used. You should run through your list of adverse conditions, and then imagine your positive responses. You should do this a few times to be completely prepared and ready for that bad event.

Even better is to implement adversity in real life. Nick Faldo, Hall of Fame golfer, followed such a principle for the 1987 PGA Championship. The contest was to be held in Florida in the middle of summer. Nick Faldo at that time lived primarily in England, and knew he was not going to be accustomed to such a high level of humidity. To prepare his body, he sat in a sauna regularly for three weeks before the tournament. He knew he had to get his body accustomed to the adverse conditions of the Florida heat if he wanted to win the championship. Nick did not win that event, but it clearly showed a winner's determination and plan of attack for an important contest.

HAVE A BACKUP PLAN

Besides having an adversity plan, success comes from having a backup plan. President Jackson was always a defender

of the Union. He was adamant against any early secession moves by the Southern states. He loudly used military
threats to quell any ideas of secession, but at the same time,
behind the scenes he produced legislation in Congress to
defuse possibilities of secession.

Always have at least two plans for any given situation.
You may fail if you have only one plan for each crisis at hand.

PREPARE FOR THE UNEXPECTED

Are you always prepared for the unexpected?

According to Mark McCormack, founder and CEO of
IMG, the agents who were prepared for the unexpected
became the stars of his company. Mark McCormack saw
many new agents rise to the top of his agency, as well as
many others who floundered. As the key decision maker in
his company, Mark would call a lot of meetings, some sched-
uled and some ad hoc. Mark mentioned that the ad hoc
meetings illustrated whether an associate was well prepared
and consistently doing her homework. McCormack stated
that the agents who anticipated the unscheduled meetings
appeared most competent, and as a result, rose to the top of
his firm much quicker than those who appeared unprepared
at those meetings.

CHAPTER ELEVEN

Wear the Red Shirt

Do you know why Tiger Woods wears a red shirt on Sundays?

Tiger Woods, the greatest golfer of our generation, does everything for a reason. Tiger surrounds himself only with people who will allow him to excel, and he sets his tournament schedule to peak during the majors. Much more than a superstition, Tiger wears a red shirt during the final round for a purpose. Putting on a red shirt makes Tiger feel pumped up and subsequently ready to play much more aggressively on Sunday.

How can putting on a red shirt make Tiger play with more fervor? How can clothing selection promote excellence?

First, take the color red. Typically, this color stands for aggression and assertiveness. As a prototypical example, the matador uses a red cape to make the bull more aggressive and charge at him.

Second, motions drive emotions. Self-perception theory states that we infer our emotions from our actions. Our brain gets the message from our body how to feel. If we act sad, we will feel sad. If we act happy, we will have feelings of joy.

In Tiger's case, the motion of wearing a red shirt drives the emotion of getting fired up. The red shirt helps Tiger feel more aggressive on Sunday and shoot low scores.

The premise of Tiger's red shirt has a huge impact on your workplace attitude. In the most simplistic of examples, wearing a red power tie will make you feel more aggressive for an important meeting (hopefully, not on Sunday). But this principle extends far beyond the clothes factor. People who act like winners feel like winners, think of themselves as winners, and are more likely to become winners than people who don't act like winners.

Unfortunately, when the chips are down, many people act like whiners, not winners. Sally Petaluma, a teacher at George K. Porter Middle School in Granada Hills, California, had this problem. She had loads of talent, and great knowledge. But when the students acted up, or spoke to her with disrespect, she would begin to act very sheepishly. She would lose her confidence and nerve to teach, and the students would take further advantage of her.

Sally was a bad actor. Her negative body language chased her confidence away. Her lack of acting skills blocked her success and prevented her from fulfilling her potential as a great teacher.

You may never take acting classes or want to be on stage or in the movies. But to unleash your work potential, you must believe in being a great actor at the right time. The following drills can help you become the actor all champions need to be.

FAKE IT 'TIL YOU MAKE IT

Fake it 'til you make it. We have all heard that cliché, but champions, like Chris Evert, do just that. She always acted confident and committed, even when she felt out of sync with her game. But Chris never revealed feelings of weakness or doubt to anyone, especially her opponents—she faked it until she made it. She kept her head high and always strutted her stuff until her game began to mesh on the court with her actions. Her exceptional acting skills helped her achieve 18 Grand Slam tennis titles.

Sure, there will be days when you do not want to be at work, or at a particular meeting. You may have not prepared well enough because of time constraints or were just not motivated to be engaged in some project. But at the same time, you must get it done, and in a very confident way. This is when you fake it 'til you make it. Become the great actor on the work stage. Your motions will create effective emotions.

SMILE, SMILE, SMILE

Getting happy can just take a smile. We infer from our upturned lips that we must be happy, and we consequently become more cheerful.

Even faking a smile will make you happier. Try it. Did you feel happier?

Duttons, a real estate company in Indiana, believes wholeheartedly in this performance principle. They have mirrors placed on their phones to remind their sales staff to smile when talking to customers. Duttons believes more sales will come when the phone attitude has more cheer.

Keep smiling at work and you will enjoy the day that much more because of your enhanced productivity.

STRUT YOUR STUFF

Do you lose energy in the middle of the day? Do you feel like you are always fighting gravity, with gravity winning?

Create more energy by strutting your stuff down the halls. Act as if you are always going somewhere important, even if you are not. Walk with your shoulders back and swing your arms with an invigorating pace. Your increased motion will increase a feeling of energy.

APS Enterprises uses this principle as one of their corporate strategies. Workers stand all day, not allowing their bottoms to meet any cushions. According to APS, standing boosts energy.

You may not want to take such as an extreme measure to boost your energy. Try this instead: Continually change your posture when talking on the phone. Try spending at least 50 percent of your time on the phone standing or moving around instead of just sitting. And when on the computer, take a break every 20 minutes and shake out your fingers and hands. This practice not only acts as a good stress reliever, but you should start to feel the energy rush throughout your body.

PLAY THE ROLE

Roger Doctrine, head football coach at Alemany High School in Mission Hills, California, would tell his players that a transformation occurred when they entered the locker room. They were no longer a student, friend, boyfriend or son—only a football player. All the problems associated with those other roles were gone. They now had to act and think only as a football player.

You could do the same as soon as you enter your car in the morning. You have entered onto a different stage: the work stage. You are no longer the husband or wife, mother or father, but the accountant, lawyer, adviser, or doctor—the working role. Allow all the problems of your other roles to be lifted from your shoulders.

Once you leave the car for the day, enter back into the role of a spouse or parent. Become completely engaged with the world again. Totally immerse yourself into your family and friends. This is not acting, but rather living!

CHAPTER TWELVE
Choose Your Attitude

Our attitude is a choice. Sometimes, we forget that simple yet powerful awareness tool. Nonetheless, one of the most difficult tasks is to keep that sweet feeling when our performance has taken the train south for the day.

The greats, however, are always the conductor of their positive emotions. Take the amusing example of Willie Mays. Willie, known as the "Say Hey Kid," had an eternal smile on his face. A former teammate recalled how one day at the start of a big game, Willie declared to the guys, "This is going to be a great day; I'm going 4 for 4. No doubt about it." Mays then went to the plate and readily struck out looking. He came back to the dugout and told his teammates, "Today is a great day; I'm going 3 for 4." When he failed to get a hit, he then proclaimed to his teammates that he was going 2 for 4 that day. Then he grounded out to third on his next at bat and proceeded to the dugout telling whoever would listen that he was going 1 for 4 on this glorious day. Later in the game, when he was robbed of a base hit on his last at bat, he smiled and said, "Tomorrow is going to be a great day. I'm going 4 for 4."

Once after a big loss by the Green Bay Packers football team, a reporter asked Coach Vince Lombardi how he was going to deal with this loss and what was he going to say to his players. Lombardi turned to the young reporter, and said, "Son, we didn't lose the game; we just ran out of time!" Now, *that* is choosing to be positive about the clock!

No matter how poorly you are performing, you can always choose to focus on the positive. It worked for Tom Watson on his victory at the U.S. Open in 1982. Most remember his remarkable chip-in on the seventeenth hole, but most important to his victory was the little known event on the seventh hole. Here, Tom missed a two-foot putt. It didn't even touch the cup. But it did not get him down in the dumps; he merely told himself that even great putters can miss an occasional easy one.

Winners like Willie Mays, Vince Lombardi, and Tom Watson know their attitude is a choice, and choosing the correct one will affect their future performance. But they have discovered nothing original. Centuries ago, the founder of modern philosophical thought, René Descartes, wrote that we have the capacity to think whatever we choose—to have thoughts that are either self-liberating or self-defeating. More recently, Victor Frankl wrote in his book, *Man's Search for Meaning*, "Every human has the freedom to change at any instant. The last of the human freedoms is to choose one's attitude in any given set of circumstances."

We have a choice to remain positive about the economy, our job, even our boss, regardless of circumstances. If you make the correct choice, then the chances are much greater that you will become more effective at your job and happier in your life. The following tip will help you become a better conductor of your attitude.

HAVE AN EARLY MORNING HAPPY HOUR

When most people wake up, they rub their eyes and then begin to think about all the tasks they must do during the day. When this list is overwhelming, and on many occasions it is, you may want to stay in bed.

Instead, choose to have an early morning happy hour. Try this exercise: when you wake up in the morning, focus on three things you are thankful for in your life. It could be your spouse, your children, your health, your upcoming vacation—focus on something that puts a smile on your face. You will find that when you make this choice, happiness will fill your cup in the early hour.

CHAPTER THIRTEEN

Fill Your Mind with Golden Nuggets

On his first job as an assistant sports editor for the *Montpelier Leader-Enterprise* in Montpelier, Ohio, Fred Bauer received an intriguing letter from a fan. He opened it and read, "Sweet piece of writing on the Tigers. Keep up the good work." It was signed by Don Wolfe, who was the well-known sports editor of the rival paper, the *Toledo Blade*.

At that time, Fred was only a teenager and getting paid 15 cents a column inch, but that letter was priceless. To Fred, it could not have been more exhilarating than to get those kind words from such a seasoned professional.

Fred kept this letter in his desk for years until it got dog-eared. When he doubted he had the right stuff to be a writer, he would reread Don's note and walk on air again. This letter paved Fred's career with golden confidence.

Joe Montana, the famed quarterback, kept a bag of gold nuggets in his head and used one to win the 1989 Super Bowl. The San Francisco 49ers were down three points against the Cincinnati Bengals with two minutes left to play.

They needed to march 90 yards to the goal line. In the huddle, Joe told his teammates "This is just like '81."

Those words in the 1989 huddle allowed Joe and the other 49ers to recall a gold nugget—a very similar pressure situation in which they had succeeded. When they were playing the Dallas Cowboys in the 1981 NFC championship game, the 49ers needed to drive the entire field in the last minutes of play. With just a few ticks left on the clock in 1981, Montana threw the famous pass to Dwight Clark for the winning touchdown. That winning image—that gold nugget—gave them a sudden jolt of energy and bolstered their confidence in 1989, which carried them to victory over the Bengals and to another Super Bowl championship.

Recalling successful experiences is paramount to developing a strong mental game and mastering your emotions. Individuals who can replay key successful moments in vivid detail have an enormous advantage against those who lack this skill.

As with Montana, numerous situations happened in your life when you scored that important business win. Most account executives can recall a presentation that went flawlessly, a textbook intro, a concise service offering, a quick negotiation, and then a mutual agreement to do business. Deposit these gold nuggets in your memory bank, and like Montana, make withdrawals when needed. In that way, you will be rich in mental and emotional toughness. Here are some additional ways to fill your mind with gold nuggets.

DEVELOP A VICTORY LOG

Sometimes our memories can fade or be suspect. So, do more than just keep these golden nuggets locked in your mind. Keep them in a victory log.

After a great event with a client (for example, a perfectly handled objection, a brilliant closing statement), record the happening in a journal called a victory log. Also, record the time and date. Refer to this journal every few days as Fred Bauer did for a quick jolt of energy and as a way to boost your confidence.

COLLECT VICTORY MEMENTOS

Be a collector of golden moments. If you inked a great transaction, have the finalized lease, purchase order, or commission check framed. Or, after a stellar business meeting, grab a token that reminds you of that moment. Perhaps it was the company pen. Keep it on your desk and allow this token to be your golden nugget of confidence. Grabbing the purchasing agent's crystal paperweight, however, is probably not a good idea.

CHAPTER FOURTEEN

Enlighten Your Game

The road to success follows many twists and turns and peaks and valleys. Everyone who has risen to the top has fallen time and time again. However, those individuals who can ride through these ups and downs with resolve are the ones who achieve success.

One of the greatest examples of resiliency is the story of Thomas Edison. While he is known as the most successful inventor of his generation (perhaps of any generation), Edison faced many obstacles and failures along the path to fortune and glory. When he started his company, the young Edison faced excessive debt from acquiring the latest and best equipment for his laboratories. On another occasion, his laboratory burnt down in the middle of night with all of this new equipment. Also, jealous employees stole his designs and infringed upon his numerous patents. The most famous resiliency Edison story, retold many times, is the number of mistakes and flops he had before discovering an effective filament for his light bulb.

Thomas Edison is the epitome of an optimist. He did not view these difficulties as failures, but rather as successes.

Edison saw a failed experiment as leading to another path. He simply saw every failure as a temporary roadblock to his future success.

Dewey Bushaw adopted a similar strategy for dealing with all of his failures along his road to success. Dewey hit the road selling Pacific Life Insurance Company products to many customers more than two decades ago. Regardless of how great a product he had to sell, many of his clients would not buy it. Dewey did not take it personally or permanently, however; he'd say to himself, "I have the right product. This is just the wrong time." This strategy filled Dewey with resiliency as well as enthusiasm. He knew that his rejections were only temporary—he believed a yes was just around the corner. Today, such resolve has led Dewey Bushaw to be the executive vice president at Pacific Life.

In sports, athletes face one failure after another. If athletes do not have an optimistic strategy, they are sure to succumb to all the negative experiences. One such athlete was the Hall of Famer Yogi Berra, who played amazing baseball for the New York Yankees. Yogi Berra didn't blame himself when he wasn't hitting, he blamed his bat. If his woes continued, he changed his lumber. "I know it sounds silly," Berra said, "but it keeps me from getting down in the dumps. It keeps my confidence up." Yogi Berra, while known for his dull wit, was actually using a brilliant strategy to build his resiliency to failure. Lumber is a lot easier to change than your ability to hit a 90-mile-per-hour fast ball.

Thomas Edison, Dewey Bushaw, and Yogi Berra are all great examples of individuals who allowed their optimism to shine on their paths to success. Most people believe that optimists see the glass as half full while pessimists see the glass as half empty. This is the archetypal analogy. Today, psychologists believe that the difference between an optimist and a pessimist is how each explains a failure event. Furthermore, the difference in how these two groups evaluate an event greatly influences future motivation, persistence, and performance.

Optimists possess a high level of resiliency because they follow what is known as the TUF strategy (Temporary, Unique, and Flexible) when describing failures. That is, when a failure comes to an optimist, they see it as temporary. For Dewey Bushaw, he saw a "no" as a short-lived occurrence. Eventually, he believed, his prospect would turn around and say yes. Also, optimists see failure as unique. An optimistic salesman would see a "no sale" as when a product does not match up well with a particular prospect, but this same product will match up well with his next prospect. Failure to an optimist is flexible. Yogi believed that if he changed his bat, success would be around the corner. Optimists believe that they can influence future events by changing their strategy. To optimists, strategies are flexible.

Pessimists, on the other hand, believe in different explanations for failure. First, pessimists believe that failure is permanent. A pessimistic salesman who is performing poorly in the first quarter will believe that low sales will continue to occur in the next quarter. Second, a pessimist believes that failure will happen for all situations. A pessimistic ballplayer, who can't hit against one curveball pitcher, believes he lacks the skill to hit against every curveball pitcher. Third, pessimistic individuals believe they have limited control over their failures. They think there is nothing they can do to avoid failure. A pessimistic financial adviser believes that no pitch will work to investors because the market controls his destiny.

The TUF strategy used by optimists appears to promote a much higher level of achievement, regardless of venue. In business, psychologists have discovered optimists were more successful in sales and had greater job retention when compared to pessimists. In the world of sports, optimistic swimmers swam faster after a failure experience than pessimistic swimmers. In academics, optimistic students had higher GPAs than their pessimistic counterparts. This apparent difference happens in health as well, with optimistic individuals getting sick less often and, more important, living longer.

The good news, for those who believe they are bit too pessimistic, is that anyone can become more optimistic about life. Martin Seligman, author of *Learned Optimism*, and the foremost psychologist in this area, indicated that an optimistic style can be acquired with the appropriate thinking patterns. Following are strategies to help you develop the TUF mentality.

TUNE UP THE T

To enhance the temporary dimension of failure at your job, you should see mistakes and lost opportunities as fleeting. See life more as a series of peaks and valleys. Some days are just going to be good and we will click with the client, and some days are going to be much worse. Some days our pitch will seem flawless while other days it will drag. There might not be an apparent reason for the difference. It is just an off day that led to awful results. Here are some examples of questions to ask yourself when you fail that will emphasize its temporariness.

- Were you at 100 percent today? (Perhaps you had a bad night's sleep.)
- Did you give 100 percent today?
- What might change in the near future, such as the economy, that could lead to different outcomes?

URGE ON THE U

To enhance the unique dimension of failure, you should emphasize how the event was special. For instance, you could focus on how the client may have not matched up with your personality, while the next client will be a better match. Or, your products were just not a great fit for the previous client. To urge on the U, address the following concerns:

- What was it about this particular client that did not work with you?
- Did you have unique feelings about this client?
- How was this situation unique? Was the product a good match?
- How do your skills match up differently with upcoming clients?

FOSTER THE F

To enhance the flexibility dimension, you should illustrate how failure can change by altering your behavior. For instance, perhaps you did not prepare enough for the meeting and failed to connect with the important client. Or, you tried a hard sell when a softer one would have been more appropriate for this particular client. To foster the "F" in your mentality, these questions should be addressed:

- Can you change any strategy for the upcoming situation to be more successful?
- What else can you control to prevent failure in the future?
- Should you seek out a mentor or adviser to guide you down a different path?

When you develop the TUF mentality, the road to resiliency should be much easier to find.

CHAPTER FIFTEEN

Be Comfortable in the Uncomfortable

Kyle Logan had prepared for a month for his presentation with Kendrick Manufacturing. He had just started his own public relations firm, Logan International. Kendrick was the big fish he had wished for. This client could get his company up and running, and Kyle knew it. He had researched Kendrick for months. Kyle then prepared what he thought was a great pitch, and then practiced it over and over until he had it down cold.

When the big day came, Kyle choked away his future. He started off fair, and then it got worse. His mind began to race, and so did his words. He began to slur one word into the next, and he could tell that the Kendrick team was getting annoyed and frustrated. From there, it went on a downward spiral to awful. Needless to say, Kyle did not get the account.

Kyle performed terribly because he did not know what his body would do under intense pressure—and this was one of the biggest moments of his life. Sure, he practiced his

presentation, but under calm conditions. He did not practice with excessive pressure, and so he did not know what to
do when his emotions became overwhelming. Subsequently,
he choked away his future.

The difference between great performers and average
ones is that they know how to be comfortable in the uncomfortable. They know what their body will do under pressure
and so they have the right response. Take a scene from the
1986 Masters. Jack Nicklaus was 46 years old and most
observers believed past his prime. He had not won a major
in six years. But Augusta National is different—the place
has magic for Jack.

On the fifteenth hole, he was four shots behind the
leader, Severiano Ballesteros, the best of the young guns for
his generation and already a major winner. Jack hit a boom-
ing drive and was only 200 yards from the green on the par
five. His caddy, his oldest son Jackie, motioned to his father
to use a 3-iron. Jack, who had been under intense pressure
conditions all his professional golfing life, knew his body and
felt the changes caused by pressure. Jack told his son that
a 3-iron would go too far—he felt the pump of the adrenaline
flowing in his veins. He motioned for the 4-iron. Jack proceeded to hit the ball on the sweet spot of the club, finishing
about 12 feet from the hole. Jack then rolled the putt in for
an eagle and went on to win, what many considered, the
greatest Masters of all time.

According to Daniel Goleman, one key component of
emotional intelligence is being aware of your emotions. All
the greats have an intuitive sense of their body and how it
will respond to the pressure. For Jack, he knew he would
hit his 3-iron over the green and possibly into the pond that
sits just beyond the green. Others have come to the same
situation and faltered. Jack is known as one of the greatest
golfers to ever play—if not the greatest—and much had to
do with his awareness of his emotions and how to control
them under pressure. Jack's emotional IQ is pure genius.

To gain an awareness of how your body will respond under pressure, you must follow the principle of situational similarity. Performance psychologists have long known that the best way to prevent choking under pressure is to create practice situations as similar as possible to performance conditions. In essence, when the practice situations mimic pressure conditions, individuals will begin to understand what their bodies do under pressure; they will consequently be prepared. This preparation allows us to have a greater transfer of skills to the performance realm.

Avoid the fate of Kyle Logan. To perform at your best under pressure, create pressure situations when you are practicing your craft. You need to learn how to be comfortable in the uncomfortable. Learn how to manage your emotions and perform at your best when the stakes are the highest. The following drills will help inoculate you against choking.

HAVE YOUR OWN REALITY SHOW

One of the greatest clutch kickers in National Football League history is Adam Vinatieri. His ability to perform in the clutch came most likely from the development of his reality show on the field. He made practice just like reality. During practice, he always kicks with his helmet on and buckled. He got team officials to pipe in crowd noise during practice. Adam times every kick he makes, from when the ball is snapped to when he launches it off the field—nothing changes from practice to the game. His reality show has helped him win two Super Bowls with last-second kicks.

Make your own reality show when practicing your skills. Regardless of the situation or who you are in the company, you will be nervous when the stakes are high. Don't deny it and practice being comfortable in the uncomfortable. If you have to make an important pitch to your colleagues, then imagine all the key players in the room. Feel the pressure when practicing. Get your heart rate up. Perhaps you could do a few jumping jacks to simulate how your heart pounds in a pressure situation. Then give your speech.

Make your practice as real as you can and your skills will transfer in excellent shape.

PRACTICE WITH CONSEQUENCES

Phil Mickelson, winner of three majors, has a golf putting drill in which he practices with consequences. He has to make 100 putts in succession from a 3-foot radius. If he misses one, he starts all over. Now, *that* is applying the pressure.

Practice with consequences when you are preparing for a presentation. Ask a few colleagues to listen in, and tell them for every mistake you make, you will hand them a crisp $20 bill. That will get them into the room as well as apply the pressure on you. While you may get a bit poorer using this process, you will be much richer knowing that you will be comfortable in the uncomfortable.

CHAPTER SIXTEEN

Pump Up with Positive Self-Talk

Billy Mills' story rings true of the Olympic dream. A Native American who grew up on a reservation, he earned a track scholarship to attend the University of Kansas. Billy had many difficulties, however, as a Native American at what was virtually an all-white school. He consequently dropped out and joined the army, where he began training for his dream, an Olympic gold medal.

Mills knew that to be the world's best in the 10,000-meter race, he not only had to train his body, but also his mind. To accomplish this goal, he kept a journal and every day would jot down positive self-statements about the upcoming Olympics in Tokyo. He wrote such affirmations as: "You are going to feel great the day of the Olympics" and "You are going to have great energy in Tokyo." Mills believed the subconscious mind and the conscious mind cannot differentiate between reality and imagination. By repeating positive self-statements, you will believe them whole-heartedly.

Billy responded amazingly well to all of his positive self-talk and self-reinforcement. In the Olympic finals, Mills was third as he came to the home stretch of the race. Then all his training came to fruition and he said to himself, "You can win, you can win, you can win." With those words came an incredible last kick, and Mills pulled off one of the greatest upsets in Olympic track and field history by coming from behind to win the gold medal.

Self-talk is actually a type of self-hypnosis. By repeating positive self-statements over and over again, Mills hypnotized himself into believing in his excellence. He created a continuously playing positive mental tape that boosted his energy when he needed it most, on the last leg of his race.

But self-talk goes beyond self-hypnosis. Our thoughts create neurological impulses in our brain, and these impulses stimulate new pathways. Repeated thoughts become stronger and more available. Positive self-talk can supercharge our emotions, making us super performers.

Unfortunately, many people fall flat from the negative mental tape playing in their heads. Dick Ross had this problem. Every time he would meet an important client or had to make a presentation to his colleagues, he would say, "Don't mess up again" or even worse, he would berate himself with the statement, "Don't be a stuttering fool again." As a child, Dick had a problem speaking because he had a stutter. Now, when he gets into pressure situations, this old mental tape gets replayed. Dick is strengthening his brain structure the wrong way with this destructive self-talk, and as a result, has never reached his potential in his field.

Do you have a negative tape continuously playing in your head? Is it hurting your performance and potential?

The following tips will help you change your tape from negative to positive.

DEVELOP A BEST FRIEND'S JOURNAL

Like Billy Mills, develop your own best friend's journal. In this journal, write a positive self-statement every day about what you want to happen. For instance, one day you would write: "I am the top sales producer in my company" or "I have great charisma." The next time, you might write: "All my business associates enjoy my humor." Keep this journal in your office and write one best friend statement each day. At an appropriate time, such as right before a big meeting, read a few entries from the past few weeks for a golden jolt of positive energy.

MAKE EVERY CLIENT YOUR FAVORITE

Jack Nicklaus has said he gets goose bumps driving up Magnolia Lane—the entrance of Augusta National. Jack has a love affair with this place and he won six Masters titles there.

On the flip side, Lee Trevino has stated that Augusta National and he were never a good fit. Lee Trevino has won every major except the Masters. Perhaps if he felt a love for the place like Nicklaus does, he might have won there.

The same principle readily applies to self-talk in business: Make every client your favorite. You can find something wrong with every client as well as find something special. Perhaps it is your client's persistence in saying no which you can see as determination. Or, your client always declaring how busy she is, which can be seen as diligence. In all cases, find something you value in each client or simply tell yourself how you admire a particular client's uniqueness. You can talk yourself into having a great attitude with any client, or talk yourself out of liking any client. The choice is yours to succeed.

BE LIKE BRUCE LEE

Bruce Lee implemented an ingenious imagery technique for ridding himself of negative thoughts. When negative thoughts would enter his mind, he visualized writing those thoughts on a piece of paper. Then, he would imagine the paper becoming a tightly wadded ball. Last, he mentally lit the paper on fire, burning it to a crisp. Once destroyed, that specific negative thought would never enter his mind again.

Be like Bruce—do not let negative thoughts burn you up or burn you out. Knock them right out of your mind.

SNAP OUT OF IT

Make a fashion statement and tie a rubber band around your wrist. Every time you have a negative thought, snap it. Not so much that it hurts, but enough to know you mean business.

If your mental tape is filled with negativity, the rubber band will continually bounce off your wrist all day long. But over time, your snaps will start to diminish and so will your negative self-talk. You can keep wearing the rubber band as a fashion statement if you wish.

CHAPTER SEVENTEEN

Get a Lifeline

Amy Miller walked into her boss's office and declared, "I don't think I have what it takes for this job." Amy had just redesigned the Park City Bridge and was six months behind schedule and $40,000 over budget. Amy then added, "I love the work. What I don't enjoy is the stress of the numbers and time constraints when trying to complete every job."

Amy works for Badgett and Badgett Associates, an architectural design company just outside Boulder, Colorado. Her boss, Tim Badgett, had hired Amy for her creative flair and spunk, greatly needed when felt was the company was losing touch with the times.

Tim Badgett has been the CEO of the company for the past 10 years. His father had stepped down a decade ago, after starting the company 30 years before. Tim knew a great personality and employee when he saw one and told Amy, "I just visited the bridge this morning—the lines and shapes fit perfectly within the contours of the environment. The bridge complements the river and molds into the mountains like no other bridge I have ever seen. It is magnificent." He added, "Amy, you are a visionary." Tim then told Amy to forget about the small details; he would have someone help her with those issues.

After the meeting, Amy wrote on a piece of paper *visionary* and posted it on her computer. She had decided to use that as her job line. She would focus on the big picture and not worry so much about going over budget or a delay in completing a project. Her job line allowed Amy to settle into a fantastic career.

Do you have a job line? Or better yet, a lifeline—a pithy statement to guide your emotions, actions, and decisions down the best path.

The all-time great tennis player John McEnroe has a lifeline: "Always moving forward." John said his desire is to continually move ahead in his life. He is always trying new things. Besides being a tennis player, John has played in a band, owns an art studio, hosted his own talk show, and currently commentates tennis matches for television. John's lifeline has guided his entire career.

GET A LIFELINE

Develop a lifeline—one that fits your goals and guides your actions.

Here are a few suggestions:

- Always keep trying
- Bounce back
- Be a visionary
- Never give up
- Be your own best friend
- Don't sweat the small stuff

Pick one that works for you and post it on the computer as Amy did, and use it as a guide as well as a comforting statement.

GIVE YOURSELF A NICKNAME

Do you remember when you gave your buddy that great nickname—that enduring name that created a special bond.

Why not give yourself a great nickname? A nickname can be a powerful tool alongside the lifeline.

When Orel Hershiser got his nickname, his career skyrocketed.

It was 1984 and Orel was struggling in the majors as a pitcher, and having a terrible season. After one tough game, Ron Perranoski, the pitching coach, told Orel that Tommy Lasorda wanted to see him in his office. Tommy was the manager of the Los Angeles Dodgers and a legend at the time. While Tommy was a passionate leader, he could also be abrasive and brash when he wanted to make a point.

At the meeting, Tommy let Orel have it. He said that Orel looked fearful on the rubber and began to berate Orel, "Who do you think these guys are at the plate? Babe Ruth? The Bambino is dead!"

Then Tommy said that Orel had the right stuff and that he believed in his skills. He told Orel that he needed to take charge on the mound, that he needed to be a fighter, a bulldog. And then Tommy said, "From now on, I am going to call you Bulldog."

Out of that meeting a nickname was born and so was a pitching legend.

Orel's nickname made him feel more tenacious on the mound and he fought for every pitch. Perhaps it's time to give yourself a nickname, one that breeds the feelings and actions you need to be more successful at key moments in your life and at your job.

CHAPTER EIGHTEEN

Think Big

Our belief system can change our physiology. Medical research has documented time after time that patients will feel better when given an inert substance, such as a sugar pill, if they are told that this pill will be beneficial to their health. They believe in the pill, and it helps their healing process. This is known as the placebo effect.

Belief in ourselves can heal any wounds of difficulty and allows us to continue with great energy and persistence toward our dreams. Rudy Kalis's belief in his abilities allowed him to overcome an unfavorable start as a sportscaster. Actually, Rudy started his television work as a newscaster in Green Bay, Wisconsin, at a small television station. By chance, the current sportscaster walked off the job because of an argument with management, and they offered Rudy a 30-day tryout to win the job. When the month was over, they brought in two consultants to evaluate his work, after which they told him that he should find a different career. Not devastated or humbled, Rudy continued on his chosen path and sent out promo tapes to other stations, one being Nashville. They liked his work, hired him, and

Rudy Kalis has been a beloved icon in Nashville for the last 30 years as a sportscaster. By thinking big—much bigger than those consultants—Rudy realized his dreams.

Belief in yourself can fuel the fire to overcome any criticism or adversity: It may even take you from stocking groceries to scoring touchdowns at the Super Bowl. Just look at the magnificent 1999 season of Kurt Warner.

After playing for his college team, Northern Iowa, for one year, and throwing for almost 3,000 yards, Kurt believed he had what it took to be an NFL quarterback. After college, he had a tryout with the Green Bay Packers. But with the likes of Brett Favre and Ty Detmer, he did not have a chance and was cut.

He moved back to Cedar Falls, Iowa, and got a job being a stock boy at a local 24-hour supermarket. He still kept his dream alive, however. He continued to prepare for his shot at the NFL, staying in shape mentally and physically, studying game film and hitting the weights. All the while, Kurt would tell his co-workers that he was much more than a grocery boy, that someday he was going to play in the National Football League.

Then he got his chance—another tryout with an NFL team, the St. Louis Rams. He had a terrible tryout, but they signed him anyway and sent him to Europe. He led that NFL Europe team in passing yardage, which opened up a spot back home as the second-string quarterback for the Rams. When an injury came to the starter, Trent Green, Kurt Warner finally had his chance.

In the 1999 season, Warner generated the second-best statistical season of any quarterback in NFL history. He completed 65 percent of his passes and 41 touchdowns. He led his team to the Super Bowl—coming from behind with a game-winning drive in the last two minutes. In that magical year, Warner was voted the NFL's Most Valuable Player, as well as the Most Valuable Player in the Super Bowl—a long way from bagging groceries—and it all came from a true belief in his ability. Kurt thought big and he achieved his ultimate goal.

While our belief system can help us accomplish wondrous achievements, it is a double-edged sword—our beliefs can also create a ceiling to our potential. This belief principle happened with the 4-minute mile. No one thought it was possible to break that impenetrable mark—and so no one did. However, amazingly, when Roger Bannister did accomplish this world-class feat in 1954, there were 45 other runners who broke the barrier within the next five years. These runners had a belief of limitation until Roger shattered it for them.

Believing in limitations could have changed our political history. Two years before the historic election of Barack Obama to the presidency of the United States, many critics said that the nation was not ready to elect a black man as president. Some pundits declared that the main limitation for this candidate was his race.

But Obama and his campaign staff did not listen. They thought big, beyond any limitations. According to David Axelrod, head of Obama's campaign, they never once had a discussion of race—how it was a weakness or how to use it as an advantage. They disregarded this apparent limitation, and focused on their key message: change and hope. Because of big thinking, we now have a president who transcends any racial barrier.

The following tip will help you to think big and overcome any belief barrier.

THINK BIG

Arnold Guten, a young financial adviser at Merrill Lynch, had a ceiling problem. He would only call on individuals whom he considered had a small portfolio to invest (under $500,000). He felt comfortable speaking and dealing with this clientele. He would never call upon clients who had over

$1,000,000 to invest and would never dream of interacting with a CEO with $100,000,000 in his portfolio. Arnold Guten thought small. As a consequence, Arnold had a business that was small. He never met his quota, and after three years, he went into a different line of work.

Have you placed a ceiling at your job? Do you see yourself making a certain salary, and that has placed you into a comfort zone of working small? Do you live smaller than your potential?

If so, smash this barrier with big thinking!

To help you think bigger, get a small index card and write, "Think big." Place it on your refrigerator or on your computer. Every time you see this card, it is to remind you that ceilings do not exist for you. You have no limitations. You can do anything, achieve your dreams, and reach the greatest heights—in your work and in your life.

CHAPTER NINETEEN

Anticipate Your Excellence

Magic Johnson, the world-class Los Angeles Laker, was said to have eyes in the back of his head. He was Mr. Showtime. Moving down the basketball court on a fast break, he knew where all his opponents were, and as such, could dish off the ball to his teammate, as if by magic.

Magic Johnson became a legend in basketball because he was an expert in anticipation. Essential in all fast-paced, high-stress events, anticipation allows us to predict the most likely situation for a given event. If we anticipate correctly, we make the best decisions with plenty of time to spare. Like Magic, the best anticipators make a difficult situation look so easy.

Another world-class anticipator was Dennis Rodman. Whether you love him for his flare or hate him for his irreverent behavior, Dennis Rodman is considered to have been one of the best rebounders in the history of basketball. While rebounding takes great agility, quickness, and fast reflexes, Rodman relied on much more than his physical abilities to dominate his competition. What set Rodman apart from his contemporaries was his mental approach to rebounding.

Sixty percent of rebounds occur below the rim, which means that positioning is more important than leaping ability. Rodman was a great rebounder because he knew where to position himself for every rebound. Rodman analyzed an opponent's shot tendency and then applied this as a strategy for determining where to position his body to get the rebound. For instance, when Rodman played for the Detroit Pistons, he had specific rebounding strategies against two of his greatest opponents, Michael Jordan and Scottie Pippen of the Chicago Bulls. Dennis mentioned that Michael Jordan had a very soft touch and the ball would come off the rim quietly. When Jordan would shoot, Dennis would position himself closer to the basket. Scottie Pippen, by contrast, had a more forceful shot: The ball would come off the rim quicker and harder if the shot was missed. When Scottie shot, Dennis would position himself farther away from the basket to grab the rebound.

Wouldn't it be great if you could anticipate all of your clients' needs and desires? Wouldn't it be wonderful if you anticipated all their queries so that you could respond magnificently?

Or better yet, wouldn't you be more successful if you could predict what your boss was thinking and what he desires from you?

In all cases, being able to anticipate any situation that arises will make you much more successful, regardless of profession. Anticipation will allow you to become a much better communicator and connecter to your clients. It will allow you to prepare a presentational style that will resonate for every client—and who does not want to advance in that skill?

Sports researchers have discovered that the best anticipators incorporate two main sources into their prediction formula: cues in the environment and the tendencies of an opponent. The following drill illustrates how you can use these two sources to become a better anticipator at work.

DEVELOP A CLIENT LOG

Predicting what a client may be thinking is very difficult. No one is a mind reader (at least no one I know), but the best way to develop an intuitive sense of others is through knowing your client.

Bob Feller, Hall of Fame pitcher for the Cleveland Indians baseball team, would keep a log of opposing batters. After each game, he would chart the likes and dislikes of the batters he faced that day. That is, he would write down what pitches they liked to hit and which ones they would avoid. To get more precise with his player log, Bob Feller would even watch the opposing team's batting practice for little tips and hints.

Like Bob, keep a log of each of your clients. After each transaction, record which actions were effective as well as which actions failed for this particular client. Be aware of the subtle cues of the interaction. Did she smile or grin when she was satisfied with the deal? Did she fidget a lot when uncomfortable? What were some of the words or phrases that your client really liked? Which words or phrases turned her off? Were there certain behaviors or gestures that your client liked or disliked?

Also, record any tendencies of your client. Does he like the soft sale? Does he like the aggressive pitch? Does he back away when forced to make a quick decision?

View your log before each interaction to create a game-winning communication style that is tailored to the individual client.

PART 3

EMOTIONAL BRAVADO

Winners have emotional bravado. They fear not. When they do face a difficult situation, they channel that energy into a positive. Winners such as Jack Nicklaus know how to turn pressure into pleasure. Furthermore, champions face their fears to reach the top of their game. They feel the fear but do it anyway. More important, heroes like John McCain often risk failure to discover who they truly can become.

Do you know how to translate fear into joy? Are you willing to fail so that you can learn from those experiences? Do you fly in the no-complaint zone?

This section sheds insight on to how we can use our fears as well as failures to propel us to the next level. From reading these chapters, you will be able to fail forward.

CHAPTER TWENTY

Squash the Grapes

Life is not fair. Take the life of Randy Pausch. Most know him as the author of *The Last Lecture*. The book is based on an actual last lecture afforded to a faculty member at Carnegie Mellon University. It was recorded and placed on the Internet and became an international phenomenon.

If you have not read the book—please read it because there are many wonderful nuggets of wisdom on each page.

As the reader discovers, Randy is dying of pancreatic cancer. He has a wife and three young children. Life is not fair.

Also, with each turn of the page, you realize how amazing Randy was as a professor. He was in the computer science department at Carnegie Mellon, and his expertise lay in virtual reality. He would get his students to develop and participate in the most wonderful virtual reality experiments. He created a contest at the end of every semester to compare the most original experiments, and the students loved the competition. The students gained so much from his mentoring that many went on to wonderful jobs in the computer programming field.

Randy Pausch died in July 2008. He was only 47, and his students no longer get the pleasure or the fortunate experience of his mentoring. Life is not fair.

SQUASH THE GRAPES

Before his death, Randy was interviewed by Diane Sawyer. There were no sour grapes in his voice or thoughts. Randy did not believe his lot in life had anything to do with being fair or not. It just was. He was the one in 32,000 people who get pancreatic cancer each year.

More important, Randy did not deal with his lot passively. He squashed the grapes. Randy created the last lecture as a present to his children so that they would remember him and be exposed to his wonderfully positive nature. He also was adamant to create a safety net for his family. I believe he wrote *The Last Lecture* for many reasons, but one being the money his family will get from the book's royalties. It has sold millions. He created a wonderful safety net for his family.

When life becomes unfair, and it will at times, take action: Squash the grapes.

CHAPTER TWENTY-ONE

Turn Pressure into Pleasure

Everyone gets nervous, you—me—even Tiger Woods and Michael Phelps. We all get butterflies when the situation is important to us. The difference is how we view this nervousness. Great athletes thrive under the pressure. They have command over their butterflies and make them fly in the correct formation. In essence, the most successful people have learned to turn pressure into pleasure.

Brandt Snedecker's perception of a tough golfing situation led to his great success. Brandt Snedecker was an All-American at Vanderbilt University and was voted Professional Golf Association's Rookie of the Year in 2007. Even as a young college star, he basked under intense pressure and even mentioned that when he misses a green, he gets excited to get up and down and make a hard-fought par. He sees it as an enjoyable challenge. Brandt turns the pressure of the moment into a pleasurable experience.

On the flip side, many amateur golfers turn a pleasurable experience into an excruciating pressure-filled moment. If they miss a green, they are worried about not getting up and down and ruining their score. They should be enjoying their day on the course, but instead are worried about what others are thinking and about their score. They turn pleasure into pressure, and subsequently, their play is negatively affected.

How we interpret the situation, whether we see it as a challenge or as a fearful endeavor, will greatly affect our emotions. Ralph Waldo Emerson knew that a twist of viewpoint can turn moments of despair into moments of triumph when he wrote, "To different minds, the same world is a hell and a heaven." What matters most is how we interpret our situation. The labels we give a situation can radically alter our mood.

Take this example. Your child slams the door on your finger while getting out of the car, but you believe by accident. How will you feel? Most likely, you will be brimming with pain and perhaps a bit of anger. But, if you believe your child slammed the door purposefully, you will be exploding with anger with very little thought of pain. Twisting our interpretation will change our emotions.

This performance principle works wonders when controlling our energy levels. Successful people label situations in ways that will increase their excitement and enthusiasm for their job. The following drills help show you how to command your butterflies to fly down the path toward excellence.

SEE PRESSURE AS AN HONOR

Players who get to make the last shot have the most pressure. But in most cases, they have earned it. The coach wants them to take the last shot because the player is seen as someone who can win the game. They are seen as gamers, and that is an honor.

Have you ever been asked to stand above the crowd? Perhaps it was to conduct a special meeting or to give the keynote at the next conference. Don't see it as added pressure, but rather, as an honor.

CREATE A STORY

Many of us work with people or situations that are toxic and drain our energy. Luckily, you can shut off this drain by reinterpreting the situation—by creating an effective story.

One client I worked with, John Ashland, an architect, wanted to be relieved from an important project. The principal owner of the project, Dr. Boyle, was acrimonious, crotchety, and driving him up the wall with his negativity and complaints.

Instead of leaving the project, I suggested to John that we make up a story about Dr. Boyle. Most important, I told John to think about this story every time he interacts with Dr. Boyle. Here is the story we created: "When Dr. Boyle was a young boy, he was fishing on the ocean with his best friend, Ed. A storm was approaching and Ed wanted to turn the boat toward shore. But Dr. Boyle refused, saying that the storm would miss them. It didn't. The storm caught them, capsized the boat, and Ed drowned in torrential waves. Dr. Boyle has lived with that torment all of these years."

As a function of this twist in viewpoint, John and Dr. Boyle's relationship changed. John began to see Dr. Boyle with compassionate eyes instead of eyes full of contempt. In turn, Dr. Boyle began to respond favorably to John and a friendship began to flourish.

Do you have a Dr. Boyle in your life? Do you have a client, colleague, or boss who is an emotional drain?

If so, create a story to decrease this drain on your energy. First, describe the person with a few basic sentences. Next, create a story about this person in a more favorable light, or from a more compassionate point of view. Most important, before you interact with this person, think about the story you created.

This story will change your perception of the relationship, and as a result, your energy drain will be plugged and you will float to success.

SHARE THE EXPERIENCE

When I was asked to develop a mental toughness segment for the TV show *Dancing with the Stars*, the pressure was on. I knew 20 million viewers would be watching and I felt the pressure to perform well. But instead of believing that I had to prove how good a sport psychologist I am, I saw the show as an opportunity to share my knowledge and expertise with the audience. Proving is about outcome—and believing you have to prove your self-worth boosts the pressure dramatically. Sharing is a joyous state, however. Believing my knowledge is a gift to the audience allowed me to thrive in the glow of pressure. My twist in perception allowed me to feel extremely calm when we shot the segment.

At certain times in a career, many business professionals will speak to an audience, big or small. Whether it is to sell a product to a client or pitch an idea to colleagues, speaking in front of groups can be very anxiety-provoking to many.

To reduce this nerve-wracking experience, twist your perception in the right direction. Do not look at the situation as proving your self-worth, but rather, you are sharing with your audience a valuable commodity. In that sense, your anxiety decreases, and at the same time, you are in step with your message.

CHAPTER TWENTY-TWO

Face Your Fears

The scene was reminiscent of the movie *The Bad News Bears*, but in this case, the sport was basketball. Stan Morrison had just been hired to coach at San Jose State University. In the previous year, the entire basketball team had walked out on the coach, and they finished the season with football and baseball players. For Stan's first year, he had no returning starters and no players who had NCAA Division 1 experience, with many of his players coming in the form of walk-ons from the general student body. His first year's team was essentially a ragtag team, put together with some shoe polish and a little glue. Clearly, they were not going to win the national championship.

Unfortunately, they were about to play a team that just had—the University of Nevada at Las Vegas Running Rebels. Under the tutelage of Jerry Tarkanian, the Rebels had become a dominant powerhouse and one of the great basketball teams of all time. This year was no different, and to many, their play had gotten even better. To say it was a mismatch was an understatement. It was as if a high school team was about to play an NBA championship squad, and many players from UNLV did go on to play pro ball.

During the pregame warm-ups, Stan Morrison looked at his team and he could see the fear in their eyes, like a deer in a truck's headlights. They were enamored by the Rebels as well as in shock with what they thought was about to occur. So Stan ended the warm-ups as quickly as he could and brought the whole team back to the locker room. There, Stan had all his players sit around in a circle and each player had to tell his greatest fears. Stan started and spoke about a time he almost drowned. Then, the first player spoke about a fear of heights and the next about a fear of losing. Then it got personal, with the next speaking about his fear of abandonment. He told a story about how his parents had institutionalized him for a year, and he wept all the while in front of his teammates. Then the next player spoke about his fear of letting his family down. He shared with the team about the time he was babysitting his little sister, only to find her at the bottom of her neighbor's pool. Holding back his tears, he told his teammates how he jumped in, pulled her out, and started CPR, bringing her back to life. These stories went on until each player on that team expressed their inner fears to one another.

From that experience, something magical had transpired. When the San Jose team entered the court again, their fear of losing had gone. They had transformed themselves into an entirely new team, beaming with courage. Perhaps the session put everything into perspective, or perhaps letting go of their fears made them realize their potential. In either regard, they were ready to take on a clearly superior team, regardless of the consequences.

Stan, who had been coaching for 20 years and been on a national championship team himself, stated that on this night, he had never seen a team play harder. They left nothing in the locker room and gave it all they had. Of course, it would be wonderful to give you a Hollywood ending, but in reality, San Jose still lost 100 to 80.

After the game, Tarkanian came over to Morrison and said, "I do not know what you said to these players, but regardless of what they do the rest of their lives, they will all be successful."

Former First Lady and philosopher, Eleanor Roosevelt, lamented that if you run from fear, if you deny its existence, it will track you down, and grow in size with each step. The players at San Jose State faced their fears and freed their inner demons, and with it, became champions, regardless of the outcome.

The following drills can help you release your fears and allow you to realize your greatest potential.

BE HONEST

What are your fears?

Are you unfulfilled and miserable in your job, yet still not willing to leave?

What is blocking you? What are you afraid of? What is stopping you from becoming a happier person?

Most likely, it is some fear you either fail to recognize or are unwilling to acknowledge. Is it your fear of failing? Not being able to support your family if you leave? Do you fear the unknown—what is on the other side of the fence?

Be honest. List your five fears and describe how they are holding you back from being happier and achieving your potential.

Fear 1. _____

How it is holding me back:_____

_____

Fear 2. _____

How it is holding me back:_____

_____

Fear 3. _____

How it is holding me back:_____

_____

Fear 4. _____

How it is holding me back:_____

_____

Fear 5. _____

How it is holding me back:_____

_____

JUST DO IT

John Wayne once quipped, "Courage is being scared to death—and saddling up anyway." Susan Jeffers wrote about this principle in her best-selling book, *Feel the Fear and Do It Anyway*. It hit a big nerve with the general public. We all have fears. We may never get rid of our fears in their entirety, and thus, we must take action and jump.

This is the exact philosophy that made Jack Nicklaus a champion. When he feels the fear, he jumps. Nicklaus has said that when the fear starts to hit him, he asks himself, "What are you afraid of?" He then reminds himself that he would not be in that position if he were not playing well and tells himself to just keep playing, fearful or not.

Unfortunately, most people avoid fear, so that fear grows. Instead, do what John Wayne suggested: When the fear comes, saddle up anyway.

LET FEAR INSPIRE YOU

When Bear Bryant was coaching the University of Alabama football team, he was once ahead by six points with two minutes remaining in the fourth quarter against a tough opponent. Bryant sent a conservative play into the huddle. But instead, the quarterback told his team that the other side was expecting a safe play, so he was going to pass and break it wide open.

His pass was caught, but unfortunately, it was by the defense. The quarterback took off after the cornerback and chased him down five yards from the goal line, and saved the game. After the game, the press told Coach Bryant that they thought Alabama did not have any true running quarterbacks, yet he ran down a speedster from behind. To which Bryant responded, "The other team's man was running for six points, my man was running for his life."

Fear can inspire you in many ways. Appropriate levels of fear can make you concentrate at a higher level. When we are afraid, the brain releases adrenaline and cortisol, hormones that can facilitate thinking and other functions such as concentration. Being fearful of losing your best client can inspire you to focus at your next meeting. (However, be careful with your fears. Out-of-control fear has been found to paralyze the mind's critical abilities.)

Another way that fear inspires you is through constructive worrying. Our fear of making a mistake, at a presentation or in a proposal, will make us check and recheck our work, making it flawless or close to flawless.

Our fears can propel us to greater heights (and speeds), when used in a positive and constructive way.

CHAPTER TWENTY-THREE

Sing the Carly Principle

Lou Brock, the all-time great baseball player, once declared, "Show me a guy who is afraid to look bad, and I'll show you a guy who can get beat every day." Lou was so right.

The human condition is to be concerned about what others think of us, and this produces one of our greatest fears—fear of looking foolish or incompetent. We have a great need to demonstrate our competence. When we believe our actions might dictate otherwise, we get extremely nervous and anxiety ridden, which can ruin our day, both off and on the playing field.

The acknowledgment of this fear is nothing new. Aesop wrote about it in one of his fables more than two thousand years ago. In this story, a father and son were taking their donkey to town to sell it. Their journey took them through a few neighboring towns. When they arrived at the first village, a group of women laughed at them because they both walked alongside the donkey instead of riding upon it. Upon hearing this, the father suggested that his son ride the donkey. When they arrived at the next village, one townsperson shouted that the son had no respect for his elders and

109

should let the old man ride the donkey. Upon hearing this, the father got on the donkey with his son. At the next village, someone commented that they were both overloading the donkey. So they decided to carry the donkey, with both feet tied to a pole. While crossing the bridge, the donkey kicked his feet loose, causing both to drop the pole. As a result, the donkey fell off the bridge and drowned. They both realized that when you try to please everyone, you please no one and you can lose your prized possessions in the process.

Being too concerned about how others think of your work can throw your career off the bridge. Hugh Everett had been a young star in the blossoming field of quantum physics after World War II. He had put forth a unique and brash idea called the "Many Worlds Theory." Simply put, this theory states that every decision we make splits off a new parallel universe from our own reality.

In 1959, he flew to Copenhagen to meet with the foremost thinker of quantum physics, Niels Bohr. However, this titan did not support his new beliefs and was very wary of his new theory. Based upon these experiences, Hugh decided to leave quantum physics for good at the ripe age of 29.

Instead of pursuing his genius, he became a consultant for a computer company. Hugh Everett died of a heart attack at the age 51, brought about by bitterness, according to his son.

Unfortunately for Hugh Everett, he did not get to see his theory pull so much weight in the field. Today, the Many Worlds Theory is considered a linchpin in the field of quantum physics, and *Scientific American* describes Everett as one of the most important scientists of the twentieth century. Everett chose to allow criticism from others to lead him into a life of sourness and decay instead of one full of joy and brilliance.

Albert Einstein, one of the greatest scientists as well as a quantum theorist, called the need to focus on the affections from others a prison. When we become so locked in to what others think, we can ruin our careers. It ruined the promising career of Hugh Everett.

Focusing upon what others think of you can destroy a career in sports as well. Ask Ian Baker-Finch. He won the British Open in 1991, but within seven years of his victory had retired from professional golf. Many factors contributed to this decision, one being his humiliating opening round of 92 at the British Open at Troon and another was missing 32 straight cuts on the tournament trail. Baker-Finch mentioned that the main straw that caused him to leave the tour was the pressure of what everyone was thinking about his poor play. Poignantly, he said, "What I would like to be able to do is to change my name, come back in a different body and go play without the pressure of being Ian Baker-Finch."

The good news is that you can break away from the tyranny of other people's opinion—it is your choice. One of the greatest sentiments of this principle was declared by Eleanor Roosevelt when she proclaimed, "No one can make you feel inferior without your consent." The following tips can help you choose wisely.

RUN YOUR OWN RACE

Even the current greats need to choose to live by the immortal words of Eleanor, especially if you are someone who takes a lot of risks in your career like Beyoncé Knowles. She started as a singer in the group Destiny's Child, moved to a solo career, and then went into movies and television. With such a high profile career, everyone can and will criticize her every move and expression. But Beyoncé has commented that she does not waste her energy combating haters: "I can't expect everyone to love what I do."

Be like Beyoncé. Focus on what you know to be worthy and right and do not allow others to make you feel inferior or less successful. Run your own race.

FOCUS ON THE NEEDS OF OTHERS

Given her beautiful voice and wonderful career, it is quite surprising to learn that Carly Simon grew up with a stutter. As a young child, she stuttered so severely that she could barely speak in public. Her stuttering became so bad that she did not want to go to school or see her friends.

Intuitively, her mother said to Carly, "If you can start thinking about other people rather than yourself all the time, you may begin to lose your self-consciousness." Her mother believed that she could beat her stuttering if she began to focus on the needs of others, and not worry so much about how others viewed her.

Those were magic words for Carly. They transformed Carly to someone who was genuinely interested in others. Not only did she lose her stutter, she became one of the most popular girls in her class.

Developing a genuine concern for others should help you break free from the mental prison of trying to please everyone. To accomplish this, ask yourself the following questions:

How did you show compassion to another colleague today?

How did you show concern toward your boss today?

How did you show compassion for someone less fortunate than you today?

How did you show concern for your community today?

Addressing these questions can help you internalize Aesop's fable and ride the donkey down your path to excellence.

CHAPTER TWENTY-FOUR

Get Rational

When Sandy Koufax first came to the major leagues, he believed that he had to be perfect to strike out batters. Sandy assumed that his pitches had to be as accurate as throwing darts. This is not true, of course. But this irrational belief in such precision caused Sandy to feel excessive pressure. Ironically, by trying to be so precise, Sandy was losing his control. Ultimately, his belief was causing a decrease in his potential on the mound.

To overcome this belief, his catcher, Norm Sherry, explained to the young Koufax that he could get batters out by widening his target. Rather than use the mitt as the target, Sandy was told to pick up Norm's body as the frame of reference for the pitch. With a wider target, Koufax no longer tried to be a dart thrower. Sandy just let it go. With this change in belief came a Hall of Fame career.

Carl Jung, the most famous psychologist this side of Sigmund Freud, once declared, "Perfection belongs to the gods: the most that we can hope for is excellence." Carl Jung is right: Being perfect is impossible. In fact, this type of thinking is irrational, and can cause undue anxiety and neuroses.

Albert Ellis took this premise one step further and developed Rational Emotive Behavior Therapy. Put simply, Ellis proposed that it is our irrational beliefs that cause us to have excessive anxiety. To reduce our neuroses, we must make our irrational beliefs become more rational or realistic. When we accomplish this process, we open our channels for human growth. The following drills illustrate how to achieve our excellence by becoming more rational in our beliefs.

RATIONALIZE THE PROBLEM

Ellis proposed a list of irrational beliefs that we typically have that block us from attaining our potential and inhibit our personal growth. These include such beliefs as:

I must be liked by everyone.

I must appear competent at all times.

I must solve all my problems, today.

Success to me is all or nothing.

Life should be fair.

It is a catastrophe when things do not work out as planned.

Do you have any irrational beliefs from this list? If so, they could be causing you undue stress and anxiety, as well as limiting your potential at work. To change your irrational beliefs into more rational ones, follow this simple three-step procedure:

1. Make a list of all the beliefs that cause you stress at work.

2. Go through the list and analyze whether these beliefs are grounded in reality. Ask yourself why this belief

is true. Ask yourself if this belief is based in fact. Sometimes this belief will be true while other times it will be based on just an opinion.

3. Ask yourself whether these beliefs are blocking your performance at work. Are these beliefs impeding your success? If they are, perhaps it is time to change and to make them more rational.

Here is an example of this process based on the irrational belief "I must be liked by everyone."

Mark Jenson was in sales for a manufacturing company and got promoted to manager because he was a superstar salesman. He took the job, thinking it would lead to his advancement and more money in the long run.

Mark had difficulties at the job, however. When making managerial decisions, Mark was too overly concerned about what his subordinates would think of him. He always questioned his own decisions: Was the workload fair? What if he told them to do a task they really did not like to do? What if he said something they did not like?

Mark never could be commanding enough and appeared wishy-washy to his employees. As a result, his direct supervisors demoted him back to sales and his advancement was put on hold.

Mark Jenson had the irrational belief that he must be fair to everyone. This belief is not grounded in reality because sometimes the workload will not be fair. Also, Mark believed that if he was not fair, he would lose his friends on the job. If they really were his friends, they would understand his dilemma for work distribution. Those worries created great stress on his decision-making and ultimately impeded his success. Most important, if Mark had come to the realization that this belief was irrational, he would still be a manager and be on his way to bigger and better positions.

Like Mark, you too may have irrational beliefs that impede your progress at work. Check to see if any of your beliefs are blocking your growth on the job. Following are a few other examples of irrational beliefs that may be obstacles to your success.

FEAR OF PUBLIC SPEAKING

Many of us have heard or read that the number one fear in our culture is the fear of public speaking. You may get overwhelmed and freeze up at every presentation, even the meaningless ones.

Why?

We are afraid of looking foolish, of appearing incompetent to others. Yet, this is an irrational fear. If we look at public speaking, we realize that most of us are not professional speakers, so expect to make a few mistakes when presenting to colleagues or clients. That is normal and commonplace. Yet, we are so guarded against mistakes, believing we will be viewed as incompetent if we do mess up.

Centuries ago, William Shakespeare wrote "Present fears are less than horrible imaginings." We believe that it will be a horrible experience if we make a few flubs, and so we allow these irrational fears to cause excessive anxiety and ruin our presentation.

The next time you are giving a speech or presentation, remember to be rational. Know that making a few mistakes is not so horrible but rather realistic for everyone.

IRRATIONAL REJECTION

The fear of rejection can also be irrational. We do not apply for that better job or seek promotion because we are afraid of failing or of being rejected. We are in ego-protection mode; we do not allow ourselves to fail and thus do not put our skills and abilities on the line. We stay within a comfort zone and never progress.

The next time you have the possibility of being rejected, ask yourself, "What is the worst thing that can happen?"

The answer may surprise you.

ACTING AS IF IT WERE LIFE OR DEATH

Dean Smith, the great basketball coach at the University of North Carolina, once said that if all the things that we acted on were truly life-and-death situations, there'd be a lot more dead people around. Dean Smith was euphemistically speaking about how we tend to exaggerate our situations. Some of us have the irrational belief that many situations in our typical day are life and death, or at least we act like they are. This in turn causes excessive anxiety.

Try this mental exercise. Recall five events in the last month where you acted as if they were life-or-death situations. For instance, you were going to be late for work so you raced through traffic, as if someone's life or death depended on you getting there on time. Or, you were running late for a key meeting, so you were rude to a colleague as you rushed by. Next, ask yourself if the need to be punctual was really that important? Were these events really life-threatening? Did you exaggerate their importance over what might actually be more important (such as your safety or the feelings of others)?

The next time these five situations occur in your life, and many will probably happen again, just tell yourself this is not a "real" life or death happening. Be rational and you will be able to stay calm and composed.

CHAPTER TWENTY-FIVE

Make Good from Bad

Out of bad comes good. Those were the words spoken by John McCain at the 2008 Republican National Convention.

As a young soldier in Vietnam, John described himself as a cocky, sometimes abrasive person, who would pick fights and make trouble just for the fun of it. John also called himself quite selfish. At that point in his life, John wondered what the world and his country could give to him. Then, a horrific thing happened. McCain was shot down over Hanoi, and captured by the Vietnamese.

As a result of his plane crash, his body was smashed into many pieces, and his captors did little to fix his broken bones. Luckily for him, McCain had comrades who fed him and encouraged him to stay strong. For the next five and a half years, he was shuttled in and out of dirty prison cells, barely surviving.

But living in a hellhole for half a decade dramatically altered McCain for the better. McCain realized how much he loved his country—for its comforts, ideals about freedom, and for its people. But more important, John came to the realization of this philosophical principle: It is not what your country can do for you that matters, but rather what you can do for your country. As John McCain put it, "I was no longer my own man—I was my country's."

Out of bad came enlightenment, a spiritual growth. Now, to McCain, life is all about service to your country—The truth of life is giving to others.

Bad events happen to all of us. Not to the extreme of John McCain's, we should hope, but we will experience our fair share of mistakes and bad tidings. Just look at what athletes have to endure, even the great ones. We think of Michael Jordan as the ultimate shot maker, yet he has mentioned that he missed 9,000 shots along the way to basketball immortality. Or golfer Tom Watson, who was known as a choker at the start of his career because he could not win the big one and he would always fold under pressure. Yet, he endured and became an all-time great, winning nine majors.

Champions in sport and life, like Michael Jordan, Tom Watson, and John McCain, have grown from bad events, and are better for it. Following are drills to help you make good from bad.

FAIL FORWARD

Out of bad comes good—with the right perspective. An ancient Buddhist proverb says, "The arrow that hits the bull's-eye is the result of a hundred misses." That perspective allowed Tommie Kay Gatlin to become a world-class speaker.

At first, Tommie Kay spoke to groups like the Lions' Club and Rotary, all for free. But she would record every speech, and afterward, analyze every word, every nuance.

As she got better, and felt like she was connecting with the crowd, Tommie Kay began to charge for her seminars—$500 for a three-hour session. She had moved on to human resource groups at big corporations. Again, she would record her every word, but now Tommie Kay would also have all of her attendees fill out a critique about her seminar. She wanted to know what they liked and disliked. She was willing to take hit after hit, and to learn from each.

Then, after about three years of working and reworking her material, one of the attendees at her seminar, who was a meeting planner at Union Bank, and asked her to speak at their annual conference. Tommie Kay hit a bull's-eye, connecting with the audience with every story and dramatic pause. All of her mistakes had taught Tommie Kay how to be a big hit. The referrals came pouring in. Today, she is a professional speaker charging upward of $10,000 a pop, with her calendar filled.

Unfortunately, most people are not willing to take direct hits to their ego and actively critique their work, time and time again. But instead of seeing mistakes and failures as negatives, we must see them as positive experiences, as a vehicle to move forward in our trade. Daria Hazuda, scientific director at Merck Pharmaceuticals, loves failures and has mentioned that a failed experiment leads to a rich source of new, undiscovered information. In her business, failures can lead to new answers and new research experiments.

Create a failing forward journal as a vehicle to help you reflect upon bad events in a more favorable light. In this journal, write down five mistakes you made at an important event (for example, a presentation, a sales closing, a negotiation). Then, examine what can be learned from such a mistake. This is just the first step, however. To hit a bull's-eye in your career, you must take action. As the legendary basketball coach John Wooden once said, "Failure is not failure unless it is failure to change."

LEARN FROM OTHER PEOPLE'S MISTAKES

To millions of Americans, he was a joke-telling bad violinist who never aged beyond the eternal age of 39. The "cheapskate" Jack Benny created the sitcom for radio. But Benny learned his classic timing from another master, Ed Wynn. Benny would watch his show and study why certain jokes worked and why others fell flat. He realized that Wynn was doing sight gags for the studio audience rather than for the listeners at home, and as a result, many jokes did not work. From then on, Benny tailored every joke on his show for the home audience and became a comic legend.

Observe others in your field. Model their successful behavior and actively learn from their failures and you will find the correct path.

CHAPTER TWENTY-SIX

Risk the Pain of Losing

Feigned or real, many sports writers pointed to the injury of Paul Pierce as the spark that helped the Boston Celtics win Game 1 in the 2008 NBA finals. Neglected in this reporting is how that injury placed Pierce on a mental pedestal. In other words, Paul Pierce was in a no-lose situation: If he played like an oaf, no one would blame him for screwing up the game. But, if he played great, as he did, scoring 15 of his 22 points in the third quarter, the injury shows how great he really is. Pierce had a positive handicap that promoted his great play, and helped the Celtics capture their seventeenth championship.

Most athletes will tell you that the most dangerous opponent is one who is sick or injured. The injury or sickness is actually a handicap that protects their ego. There is no detriment to their self-esteem if they lose. When there is no cost to your ego, there is no holding back—it is full throttle ahead, and you become a danger to everyone.

Some individuals handicap themselves, purposely. One such example was the nineteenth-century French chess champion Alexandre Deschapelles. He was a world-class player, but had great insecurities about his abilities. As a result, he decided that he would play an opponent only if that person would remove one of Deschapelles's pawns and then make the first move. Thus, he would not look like a fool if he lost. He would claim that he had a disadvantage from the start. If he won, this handicap would show how superior he was. His self-handicapping strategy supported his fragile ego.

Regardless of profession, many people are just like Deschapelles. Our egos are like egg shells—easy to crack. We do not want to be thought of as a failure, and will thus engage in some type of behavior that protects our ego. Self-handicapping is all about protecting our self-esteem.

You have probably met many individuals at work who use a self-handicapping strategy. When a big proposal or presentation is on the line, they have a tendency to blow it off or give it very little effort. Or they continually make a variety of excuses that block their ability to put forth the effort. Then, when they fail, they can blame it on their lack of effort or excuses. But, more important, if they do succeed, they believe they will look that much better given their limited push.

Do you engage in any self-handicapping strategies? Do you engage in destructive strategies to protect your ego? The following drills will bring realization to this common but difficult problem.

THE ACT OF QUITTING

The act of quitting is a self-handicapping strategy. John Daly, winner of two golfing majors, has mentally quit a number of times in competition. Giving up protects the ego because the person does not risk all they have so they can win or play well. Athletes from all sports have stated that the pain of losing is much greater than the thrill of victory. The pain to the ego is great when we try and do not succeed.

To John Daly, his behaviors may be buffering that pain, but sadly, they are diminishing his greatness on the course.

Have you quit on anything that is important to you?

Have you quit on your dreams?

Do you realize that quitting is buffering you from this pain?

SET REALISTIC GOALS

Pain increases when goals are unrealistic. While many self-help books suggest setting high goals, these can be destructive to our self-esteem. For instance, if quotas are set too high, you may commit an act of self-destruction (for example, leaving a profession or giving up on a project) as your self-handicapping strategy.

Set goals that are reachable. Not only will you get a boost when you reach them, but you will also not produce any obstacles to block your way.

LAY IT ON THE LINE

Hale Irwin, winner of three U.S. Opens, has stated that playing competitive sports is akin to standing naked in front of a big crowd where everyone can see all your faults. Many individuals will try to cover up by self-handicapping. Those people who are not ashamed of failing and are willing to lay their ego on the line, however, are the ones who are more likely to achieve their potential.

CHAPTER TWENTY-SEVEN

Fly in the No-Complaint Zone

In 1947, Walter O'Malley was about to conduct an experiment that would rock the sports world and change the face of baseball. He signed Jackie Robinson to play with the Brooklyn Dodgers. O'Malley knew how tenuous the race situation was in America at this particular moment but he also knew his team needed a ballplayer who was not only great but could also handle the pressure of breaking the racial barrier.

As they spoke about what may happen in his future, Walter O'Malley told Jackie that every racial epithet would be thrown at him from the stands. He would have to ignore it and not complain. The opposing team and sometimes his own teammates might say derogatory remarks about his skin color. He had to ignore the worst and not complain to the coach. The umpires might make the worst calls he had ever experienced. He would have to endure it all without a murmur.

If he were to let all these things affect him, though, by fighting opposing teams, running into the stands and hitting fans, the experiment would be over, and baseball might not see another black player for a long time. Ultimately, O'Malley was asking Jackie to fly in the no-complaint zone, at all times.

All of those events did occur, but Jackie did not let any of it bother him. He had a lifetime batting average of .311, was voted the National League Rookie of the Year in 1947 and National League Most Valuable Player in 1949, and was a six-time All-Star in his 10-year career, amazing statistics for an amazing situation. Jackie Robinson was a man of honor, never complaining and ultimately, he became a legendary figure in the game of sports and baseball. The so-called O'Malley experiment was a success.

Winners can withstand the storms of their lives, without complaint. This is the philosophy of Herb Gottmer.

Herb had a local grocery store that had been in the family for 70 years on Canal Street in New Orleans. Hurricane Katrina tried to change that. When the storm hit, the entire store was flooded. All the shelves were ruined. The refrigerators broke. The place was devastated.

As we know, Herb was not unique. Most stores on his block, and many other blocks, were hit hard or simply wiped out by the hurricane. Many of the store owners complained about how there was little government help and how hard it was to get supplies back into their stores.

Not Herb—he flew in the no-complaint zone. He had to drive his own truck two hours to Baton Rouge for his supplies because his suppliers would not deliver his goods. But Herb did not complain. He did what was necessary to get the store up and running again. It took months of cleaning the floors and scrubbing the walls to get rid of the mildew. There was little help from the government or other store owners, but Herb did not complain. Herb knew complaining did no good if the family store was to get up and running again.

Today, Herb has a thriving business again in New Orleans, while many of the other stores are still closed. The locals know they can rely on Herb when it counts the most.

Both Jackie and Herb became hugely successful because they flew in the no-complaint zone. The following advice may help you follow their lead.

WEAR AN EMOTIONAL SUIT OF ARMOR

Some environments are like combat zones out there—full of complainers waiting to pierce your attitude with their negativity—they will complain about their lack of respect, their small paycheck, and their "too much work and too little time" problem.

Their complaining is bleeding their energy and driving them to misery. Just look at their body language when they complain—their heads will drop and their shoulders slouch. They frown with each word. Complaining does nothing productive for them but rather only promotes destruction of their mind and body.

Protect yourself from their negative hurricane. Wear an emotional suit of armor. Visualize a sphere around your body on all sides. This is your emotional suit of armor that allows you to live in a no-complaint zone. Complaints from others just bounce right off this armor. Wearing this armor makes you impervious to all the negative energy that surrounds you at work. Also, you cannot complain while wearing this armor. No complaints can enter or exit your emotional suit of armor.

Remember—nothing ever legendary occurred from complaining.

CHAPTER TWENTY-EIGHT

Develop Positive Rituals

Rituals are rampant in all walks of life. Some people have called them superstitions, but a ritual is some thought or behavior that is repeatedly conducted before a specific event. Some are a bit crazier than others. Some of us avoid stepping on cracks while others tap on the outside of the airplane as they enter.

Some of the strangest rituals come from sports. In tennis, Bjorn Borg never shaved during his Wimbledon days. Borg believed the extra whiskers would give added power to his ground strokes.

One of the greatest players with legendary rituals was Wade Boggs. A Boston Red Sox legend, Wade had a unique idiosyncrasy with chicken. Wade liked to eat a chicken dinner before each game, believing he would play better with fowl in his insides.

Boggs is not the only athlete who believes in the power of chicken. David Toms ate a chicken dinner from Chik-fil-A before his first round of the 2001 PGA championship. He played wonderfully and continued to eat a chicken dinner from Chick-fil-A before each round. His ritual worked and he outdueled Phil Mickelson to win his first major.

Rituals may even make us smarter. Ken Jennings was the big winner on the TV quiz show *Jeopardy*. He won a record $2.5 million and stayed on the show for five months before losing. To ensure his victory on the show, he participated in a few lucky rituals before going on stage. He stayed in the same motel and then drove his Dodge Neon rental car the same route to the Culver City Studio. He also ate the same breakfast of chocolate doughnuts every morning.

Was it the chicken for David Toms, the whiskers for Borg, or the doughnuts for Ken Jennings that contributed to their great success? Or, were these just silly behaviors?

While these behaviors may seem strange, they provide a purpose for the user. Life is very unpredictable. We want control where there is none, and rituals give us a greater sense of control. By engaging in this action, (for example, eating chicken or not shaving), we believe we have a greater influence over our lives and a specific outcome. By not shaving, Bjorn Borg felt he would play better.

Furthermore, this perceived sense of control derived from our rituals can give us peace of mind and a more relaxed attitude. By eating chicken every night, David Toms felt more at ease when he got to the course. More important, this feeling of calm can make us perform better. So the chicken dinners were very effective, in an indirect way.

Rituals are beneficial. We desire consistency and control, and rituals provide both to us. The following drills are examples of some rituals to advance your game in life and business.

HAVE START-OF-THE-DAY RITUALS

If you listen to the captains of industry, or any successful performer in the business world, they all have consistent daily routines that drive their success. Tim Rory, an architect for Morgan, German, and Lowe, has daily routines to keep his mind focused and his energy levels high. Tim gets up every morning at 5:00. He makes a list of priorities he plans to accomplish. Then he puts on his workout clothes and goes to his fitness club where he works out for one hour, and then showers. He is at his office by 6:30, ready for the day. This morning ritual gets his body and mind prepared for the everyday stresses of the office.

Do you engage in start-of-the-day rituals to get you ready for the stressors at the office?

DO NOT CHANGE RITUALS BECAUSE OF CIRCUMSTANCES

Jimmy Johnson knows what it takes to deal with the highest level of pressure, and one key is not changing your practice situations because of the importance of the next game. To prepare the Dallas Cowboys football team to play in the 1993 Super Bowl game against the San Francisco 49ers, Jimmy mentioned that his approach during practice those two weeks before the big game did not change. The Cowboys followed the same daily regimen. They made no special allowances for meeting times. Practice was the same length. The same amount of time was spent for walk-through practices as well as the time spent watching game film.

Follow Jimmy's lead—do not change your rituals before a big meeting. Prepare as if it were just another event. If you do change certain aspects, this is telling your body that something is unique, and the pressure will mount and anxiety levels will soar. Keep everything the same and you will find a calmness in the midst of the storm.

PREVENT JET LAG

Jet lag can be very destructive to productivity and can take days to recover from. Developing certain ritualistic behaviors will help you prevent or possibly recover from jet lag more quickly. Some jet lag preventive behaviors should include:

Drinking lots of water before the flight

Setting your watch for the new time zone as soon as you board the plane

Adapting to the local eating and sleeping patterns the day you arrive

Keeping up your exercise routine during your trip

Getting 12 hours of sleep the day of your return to help your time clock recover

AVOID NEGATIVE RITUALS

Sometimes we develop negative rituals because they helped us once or twice. This is a form of operant conditioning. If we got rewarded just once, we may stick with a behavior that is self-destructive. This happened to Holly Atwater when she was a gymnast in college. She did not have breakfast before her best meet, so she stopped eating breakfast before every subsequent meet. Holly has carried this ritual over to workdays, not eating breakfast before important meetings. It is unwise, however, to neglect the most important meal of the day. Even doughnuts can help with the start of your day; at least Ken Jennings believes in them.

Do you have any rituals you engage in before important meetings or confrontations? Ask yourself whether they are healthy or harmful. If harmful, then relieve them from your repertoire and find some new rituals that are wiser.

CHAPTER TWENTY-NINE

Kick the Anxiety Habit

Sarah Molton always wanted to be a defense lawyer. She saw herself as someone defending the little guy, and believed this career would help her fulfill her destiny. Sarah went to all the best schools, eventually graduating from UCLA Law School, from which she landed the plum job of working for the prestigious law firm of Allen and Allen.

The policy at Allen and Allen was to have a senior partner mentor the first-year attorneys. John Gruster, one of the partners, was assigned to Sarah Molton. John came from a stern childhood and believed that young lawyers would do best if given a load of criticism—that they would learn and grow faster from this type of feedback.

After her first trial, Sarah was invited to Gruster's office for some mentoring, where he readily told her of the many mistakes she made. Sarah, who was always very confident in her abilities as a lawyer, took his criticism to heart. After the next trial, Gruster did the same thing. After the third, he was the most critical, explaining to her the many relevant cases she forgot to mention during the trial.

After the third such mentoring session, Sarah noticed a distinct change in her feelings toward litigation. She went from feeling relaxed and joyful as she entered the courtroom to nervous and distraught. Regardless of her sense of competence for her current case, she began to feel extreme anxiety at her job but did not know why. She felt an overwhelming sense of doom every time she entered the courtroom. Sarah also began to forget some of her best material in the courtroom. As such, she decided to take a break from her law practice and reevaluate her career choice.

This same phenomenon can happen to elite athletes as well. They can condition themselves to get nervous before a game, regardless of ability level or confidence. It happened to Bill Russell. Known as one of the best team players in the history of the game, Russell won more championships with the Boston Celtics than any other player in NBA history. Yet before most games, Russell would throw up. This action became a habit. Russell conditioned his body to be extremely nervous before every game, regardless of confidence level.

How can two extremely confident people develop such feelings of anxiety?

The principles of classical conditioning can explain how Sarah and Bill can both have effective thoughts, yet have inappropriate emotions. Classical conditioning was discovered more than one hundred years ago by the Russian scientist Ivan Pavlov. In his famous experiment with dogs, he paired the ringing of a bell with the presentation of food. After a number of pairings with the bell, Pavlov discovered that if he removed the food, the ringing of the bell alone would produce saliva in the mouths of the dogs.

Human beings follow these same principles: We get conditioned from continually pairing our bodies with certain responses. For Sarah Molton, she continually paired extreme criticism of her abilities with going to trial. As a result, regardless of how she felt about any new case, or how confident she was about winning the case, she would have overwhelming feelings of dread. Her senior partner's comments had conditioned her body in a negative way. The same can be said about Bill Russell. When Bill was younger, he felt nervous before basketball games. He subsequently trained his body to be nervous. As he got older, those feelings of nervousness did not subside.

The bad news is that changing our thinking patterns may not be effective. The good news is that these feelings can be unlearned by reconditioning the body with the appropriate techniques, which are described in the following drills.

RECONDITION YOUR BODY WITH SYSTEMATIC DESENSITIZATION

One of the best methods to recondition anxiety or a phobia is with the educational technique called systematic desensitization (SD). This is a high-profile name for a simple process in which you visualize anxiety-provoking images while you are relaxed. The underlying principle of SD is that the relaxation response is stronger than the anxiety response (this is a very key point) and as such, when you pair those two responses together, the relaxation response wins, and your anxiety will be reduced.

SD works in three easy steps. First, you need to develop a scene that is producing this anxiety or dread. This scene should be composed of a sequential list of actions, with the images going from least anxiety producing to most anxiety producing. If Sarah Molton were to employ SD to help resolve her anxiety issues, her list may go as follows:

She drives up to the courthouse

She gets out of her car with her briefcase

She is walking toward the courthouse

She enters the courthouse

She enters the courtroom where the trial is set

She sits in her chair waiting for the trial to begin

The case begins

In the second step, the individual gets relaxed. Here, you can employ progressive relaxation (PR). First, get into a relaxed seated position. Then take five deep breaths from your diaphragm. Next, visualize relaxing your muscles from the ground up. Specifically, you tell yourself to relax your toes, your calves, your thighs and move up until you relax the top of your head. You do this visualization in conjunction with your deep breathing. This part to the technique should last about five minutes.

Once you have achieved this relaxed state, the last step is to visualize the sequential list, moving from the least anxious images to the most anxiety-producing ones. For Sarah, she would visualize these scenes as if she were actually there, living it, breathing it, and feeling it. The more vivid the imagery, the better it will work.

SD is an extremely powerful tool for decreasing a wide variety of anxious feelings and phobias. It can be used to reduce the fear of flying, the fear of public speaking, or any situation that produces a feeling of dread or doom. Furthermore, SD is a skill: The more you practice it, the better SD will work to help you achieve your ideal state of performance.

COOL OFF THE PRESSURE

In the book *Think Like Tiger*, John Andrisani describes how Tiger Woods enters into a calm state through a series of eye blinks. According to Andrisani, Tiger's sport psychologist taught him to associate eye blinks with relaxed feelings, thereby producing a self-hypnotic state of supreme calm and focus.

While true or not, this same procedure can help you attain a very relaxed state under intense conditions. However, instead of eye blinks, an easier technique is to use a mantra (a repeated word). More specifically, as described in the relaxation drill, you would first get into a relaxed state using PR. Once that state is achieved, you repeat a mantra with every breath. The word should be monosyllabic, such as *cool* or *smooth.* You say this word every time you breathe out.

Going back to classical conditioning principles, this word becomes associated with a calm state. Of course, it would take time to accomplish this phenomenon, but in as little as two weeks, you can learn to produce a powerful calming effect.

Here is the kicker. When you have those feelings of anxiety or doom, just breathe out and say your mantra a few times. You will find that your anxiety will be pushed aside; remember, the relaxation response is more powerful than the anxiety response. Once you learn the relaxation response, your anxiety will lose every time.

PART 4

EMOTIONAL CONNECTEDNESS

Champions like Michael Jordan have mastered the emotional strength of being connected to the present moment. They have learned to live fully in the present and focus their attention on the target, pure and simple. Winners like Olympic track star Carl Lewis know when to be engaged but also can stop thinking too much so they can perform at the highest level. They just react and let go.

Do you wonder why you can become so easily distracted at meetings and at the dinner table? Do you have a problem of letting go of past events so they creep into the present? Are you better at reacting and trusting your gut than over-analyzing something?

This section teaches you how to live fully in each moment, and when you learn that essential skill, your moments will get that much sweeter.

CHAPTER THIRTY
Zen and the Art of Business

Phil Jackson is known as the Zen Coach of basketball. He drew from Native American religions and Buddhism to help guide the Chicago Bulls to six world championships and the Los Angeles Lakers to three consecutive titles. In his book *Sacred Hoops: Spiritual Lessons of a Hardwood Warrior*, Coach Jackson describes how he encouraged his players to follow the principles of Zen and live in the moment.

One of Jackson's most famous pupils, Michael Jordan, took this philosophy to heart both on and off the court. Being in the moment helped Michael stay passionate about playing hoops throughout his storied career. Michael Jordan noted that being purely wrapped up in the moment empowered him to play basketball without any self-criticism or inhibition of any kind. When he played, he did not worry about losing because failure exists in the future, decreasing any pressure. His past did not exist either, which made the sting of missed shots quickly disappear. By living in the now, Michael could steer all his energies toward his greatness.

The philosophy of Zen can also lead to excellence in business. One leader in the financial world who follows such an approach is Suze Orman. Wearer of many hats—CEO, author, speaker, TV star—Suze Orman has mentioned that she usually does 12 different tasks every day to help sustain her company and her business empire. Poignantly, however, she stated that she focuses on only one task at a time. Orman's focus is purely wrapped into that one venture, not the other 11. Her Zen-like mentality has helped her achieve immense success.

Do you wonder why it is so difficult to live in the moment at work as Michael Jordan did on the basketball court? Do you question why you cannot concentrate all of your energies on one task like Suze Orman? Do you wish you could be more emotionally connected in your life?

The answer may lie in your concentration habits. Many of us practice being distracted. Take David Cook as a prime example. He lives the life of the everyday multitasker. At the office, he usually talks on the phone to one client, while he monitors another client's account on his computer. At the same time, he contemplates what will be said on his next phone call.

Then, when David gets home, his wife begins to talk about her day. But David parks his thoughts back at work, to the three phone calls he forgot to make. When David's son starts talking about his soccer playoff game this weekend, his thoughts jump into the future; he wonders how to rearrange his travel schedule to make that key game.

David has trained himself to become emotionally disconnected from his moments. Now when David is talking to clients on the phone or during a face-to-face meeting, his mind wanders. His clients are aware of this problem, and some relationships have soured because of it. Ultimately,

David's habit of multitasking has made him less effective in his fast-paced business world.

Are you just like David?

The great Olympic hurdler, Edwin Moses, once said, "You develop concentration in training. You can't be lackluster in training and concentrate in a meet." As with David, most of us are lackluster in our concentration training. In fact, our concentration habits can become our enemy. Instead, we need to invest in the now. To be successful, we need to take care of the moments, to immerse ourselves in the particulars. There is an old Buddhist saying, "When an individual tries to catch two birds with one stone, he usually ends up not catching any." The following drills illustrate how to capture the heart of the moment.

DO THE DISHES

The skill of being in the moment necessitates practice. In his book *Peace Is Every Step*, Buddhist master Thich Nhat Hanh proposes a mental exercise to develop such a skill. It concerns doing a mundane task: washing the dishes. The next time when you are washing the dishes, don't rush through them. Immerse yourself in the moment. Feel the warm water on your hands. Notice the rhythm of your hands. Observe how the bubbles in the water glow and have their own magic. Feel the texture of each dish and appreciate its artistry. Enjoy the simple action of doing dishes. When fully engaging in a mundane task like washing the dishes, you will find it much easier to focus when the event seems less humdrum and more meaningful.

DEVELOP A TRIGGER SENTENCE

Habits can be weakened with wiser responses. The right words at the right time have proven to be wise methods to enhance better focus for my clients.

Charlie Glenn, an office manager, came to me because he had a very difficult time letting go of problems. His mind would be cluttered with distracting thoughts throughout his many meetings.

We decided to implement a trigger sentence to enhance his ability to become more emotionally connected to the moment. Charlie was a former high school pitcher and loved the movie, *For the Love of the Game*. In this movie, Kevin Costner plays the role of an aging major league pitcher who has a unique gift. When he says the phrase, "Clear the mechanism," he can completely block out any distractions. As soon as he says those magical words, all the fans fall completely silent. More amazingly, all he can see is the catcher, batter, and umpire, as if they were placed inside a tunnel.

Charlie decided to use the same catchphrase. Whenever Charlie found his thoughts parked in the past, he would say, "Clear the mechanism." Eventually, this personalized trigger sentence helped Charlie develop the habit of being fully engaged in the present moment.

Create your own catchphrase. It could be, "Clear the mechanism," or something more personalized. Whenever you want to focus, at home or at the office, simply say your phrase. Eventually, you will override your poor concentration habit and replace it with one of full engagement. A simple sentence can be a smart, easy way to improve your concentration.

SAVOR THE MOMENT

Try this exercise: Get a Starburst or some other flavorful candy. Unwrap the candy, place it into your mouth and then close your eyes. You will be amazed by the intensity of the flavor.

Moments in time are like that: When we are fully engaged, the moment is that much sweeter.

Quiet the Mind

When the great Olympic track star Carl Lewis stepped into the blocks, he would first analyze what he wanted to accomplish in the next 100 meters. His main focus was thinking about the best way to push off the blocks. He also wanted to stay within himself down the lanes. But once the starter's gun went off, Carl would quiet his mind and let his body just fly down the track. He would let his body do what he had trained it for all those years, and his body responded magnificently with six Olympic gold medals.

When we perform at our best, we are in the reactive state. Sport psychologists have discovered that those individuals who find the Zone have literally turned off the left, or analytical, side of their brain. On the other hand, when we think too hard, we can become paralyzed by our thoughts. This is known as "paralysis by analysis" and ruined the once wonderful career of Ralph Guldahl.

In the late 1930s, Guldahl sat as king of the golfing world. He had won three majors—the 1937 and 1938 U.S. Opens and the 1939 Masters. Given his dominance, a publisher asked him to write an instructional golf book. The problem was that the game came very easy to Ralph. So, during the winter break, he set a mirror up in his house and broke down his swing piece by piece. At the end of the break, the book was finished, but so was his swing. Ralph went from no-thinking to over-thinking and his game fell off the world.

Branch Rickey, a former owner of the Brooklyn Dodgers, brought this principle to light when he declared, "A full mind is an empty bat." When we fill our mind with too many thoughts, we cannot swing. The following drills will help you to have a full bat, but a quiet mind.

TAKE A SHOWER

One of the greatest thinkers of all time, Leonardo da Vinci, once mentioned that to make your judgment clearer, we must go away every now and then and take a little relaxation.

What is more relaxing than a warm shower?

Many people will tell you that their best ideas come in the shower when they were thinking about nothing. They were just relaxing. Can lathering up really make you a genius?

In many cases, when we are struggling with an answer, we can't seem to find any in sight. We become more creative when we just let go. Sometimes, all we need to do is take a step back for a while and allow our analytical mind to shut off and our creativeness to shine through.

The next time you are struggling with a problem, put it away for a few hours, perhaps days. Take a few warm showers, get relaxed—you never know what might pop up in all that lather.

TRUST YOUR GUT

You have probably heard the phrase "Trust your gut." In a way, this implies that you must quiet your mind and just react to the situation—just make a decision based upon your initial reaction. Educational psychologists have discovered that when students take tests, they have a tendency to second-guess themselves and change their answers. Their initial answer, however, was typically the correct one—they should have trusted their gut and just reacted to the question. In most cases, our initial reaction, our gut, our nonanalytical mind, will have the right answer.

When the answer has become muddied and convoluted, go back to your initial reaction to the situation. Just react and trust your gut.

GO UPSIDE DOWN

Brainstorming events at work can get stifled because people tend to overanalyze a problem or situation. Try this exercise to illustrate the importance of shutting off the analytical mind so as to have greater creativity and greater insight into a problem. Get a simple picture that any one can copy freehand. Make two identical copies. Now, with the first copy, turn the picture upside down and draw the picture as is. Do not rotate the picture in your mind. Also, ignore anything recognizable in the picture, just draw the lines and shapes as you see them.

Once you finish with the first picture, begin to copy the second drawing. But in this case, view it right side up. Once you finish, compare the two.

In most cases, people will find that the first drawing is much more artistic and creative than the second. With the first drawing, you just let yourself draw—you shut off your analytical mind. In the second, most people are in the analytical mode, making sure their picture mimics the copy. They are in the protection mode of their ego, not wanting to look foolish. In this processing mode, we lose our creativity.

Apply this same principle to the company brainstorming sessions. First, have members of the group propose every idea related to the problem. Make sure the group does not evaluate any idea on merit or worthiness until all of the ideas are exhausted. Protect everyone's egos in the group, making sure no ideas are ridiculed. Pixar, the computer animation company, takes this approach when making a new film. When first discussing creative ideas about the film, there is a safe time when everyone is free to offer ideas—no ideas are dismissed. Given their creative success, this must be a key facet in their process.

When all the ideas have been pitched, turn on the analytical mode of the group. Decipher which ideas work and which ones fall short. Being highly critical at this juncture is the key to the brainstorming process.

Most people cannot flip themselves upside down when working on problems (although that might be interesting). However, using techniques to turn off the analytical mind will help your business stand above the rest.

CHAPTER THIRTY-TWO

Develop a Post-Event Routine

In 1992, I was fortunate to attend the University of Florida to begin my doctorate in human performance. Also fortuitous was that Lisa Raymond played tennis for the Gators at that time. Being a tennis fan, I watched Lisa and the Lady Gators play many of their matches.

Lisa played Number One for the Gators and was clearly head and shoulders above most of her competition from other schools. While her physical skills were dominant, it also became apparent that she conducted herself on the court differently from her competitors. After the point was over, Lisa went through the same routine time and time again. As an example, when waiting to return a serve, Lisa would look at her strings, take a few studder steps, and then take some deep breaths. Interestingly, her competitors rarely exhibited such consistent behavior between points.

Lisa Raymond proceeded to win both the 1992 and 1993 NCAA woman's single championships. She has since gone on to win four singles titles as a pro as well as won all four majors in doubles competition.

Jim Loehr, a sport psychologist to some of the greatest tennis players, discovered that the behaviors following the end of a point were the most crucial to tennis success. Moreover, Loehr discovered that tennis players who spent their time with a consistent routine played their best under pressure, whereas tennis players who varied their routines were more likely to choke under pressure.

Furthermore, according to Loehr, a consistent routine lowers the heart rate (HR) to an effective level. Lower HR helps players to get refocused and let go of negative thoughts. In addition, energy levels are enhanced. With lower HR, players can play harder for longer periods of time.

In contrast, players with inconsistent behaviors are hurt because their HR is throttling too high for too long. With a higher HR comes a decrease in energy, which can lead to a decrease in performance for longer matches. Inconsistent routines create choking because players do not manage their physiological responses effectively.

While business professionals may not have to work on getting their heart rates down very quickly, they will benefit from what transpires between meetings. A poor performance or failed event at the start of a series of sales calls can lead to anger and frustration for the rest of the day.

To prevent this continual downward spiral, you need to incorporate a post-event routine after each meeting. A post-event routine is a series of effective thoughts and behaviors after an event. More important, these thoughts and behaviors will put the executive back on a positive track following a negative event.

On many days, a salesperson or professional may have upward of five meetings per day. If we do not engage in any procedure following a bad event, we are doomed to let those events creep into our current situation. We need to evaluate what just happened so that we can move on to the next situation with a clear mind and heart. The post-event routine will help you let go of the past and get refocused for the future.

The following is a post-event routine based on Loehr's system that incorporates the three R's.

RELEASE

After a poor event, you must release any negative energy that has built up in your system. Ken Flach, winner of the U.S. Open, Wimbledon, and Olympic Gold medal in tennis doubles, would walk up the doubles alley after every point. He would never walk down the middle of the court to retrieve the balls. According to Ken, this series of actions helped him release any pent-up frustrations from the previous points.

While you may not be able to walk down a court following a client interaction, you can still use a release technique to your advantage, especially after meeting with a very difficult client. This can be accomplished by taking deep breaths or making a tight fist for three seconds and then opening your fist while seeing the energy dissipate. These are just a few suggestions for a release mechanism. Find one that works for you.

REIMAGE

Billie Jean King had a different routine between points. During her changeovers, she would use that time to reevaluate and visualize what she had to do next. This action, she believed, would allow her to take control of her matches.

For your meeting, do the same as Billie Jean. Reevaluate what happened and visualize what could have been done better. This will allow you to let go of the past and focus on the present, which leads to the next stage of the routine.

RESET

The last stage of a post-event routine involves resetting your mind and body for the next task at hand, which could be imminent. The reset procedure could simply be a self-statement such as "next client." When said, the salesperson is no longer parking his thoughts in the past but rather spending all of his energy on the next client. Or, it could be a statement such as "refocus." Find one that fits your needs and use it in your routine.

Mark Twain once quipped that golf was a good walk spoiled. It will be a good walk spoiled only if you let the bad shots ruin your day. Your days in business will be a good day spoiled if you allow previous bad events to seep into the rest of your day. The post-event routine is one of the most important strategies that can contribute to you having a great day, unspoiled by the past.

CHAPTER THIRTY-THREE

Open the Gates of Your Concentration Reservoir

Johnny C. was the best punter in the Southeastern conference in the late 1990s. He mentioned that one of his key weapons was not only his great skill of hang time, but also his ability to peak his focus at the key moments. More specifically, he learned how to become completely engaged at the moment of his kick. Johnny intuitively knew that if he focused for the entire game, he would drain his mental energy and not punt well. Instead, he would goof off and just enjoy the crowd and the game until it was third down for the offense. Then, he would change his focus to another gear. When it became fourth down, and he knew the coach was going to call for a punt, Johnny cranked up his focus one more notch. Then, as he jogged on to the field, he switched his focus to the highest level, made his punt, and when the play was over, he began his goofing-off process once again.

He repeated this focus procedure throughout the game, to remain fresh and consistent.

Drew Simmons would be more successful and happier if he followed a procedure similar to Johnny's. Drew owns a flag business in Indianapolis and his company customizes flags for businesses and special occasions. Although Drew works hard, he struggles with the lack of mental energy that he has left in the tank for his family when he arrives home. Because of his inability to manage his concentration levels, Drew feels out of balance.

Drew's daily routine typically consists of calling new clients, maintaining his relationships with his current client base, and managing his staff. He typically spends most of his concentration energy in the morning, managing his staff and making cold calls to new clients. His afternoon routine mainly encompasses making calls to his existing client base, which he feels is the most essential part of his job, and so he saves it for last. By that time of day, however, he is mentally drained and only spends about 30 quality minutes in this mode. As a result, Drew believes his company has begun to flounder.

We discovered that Drew's problem stems from his lack of a concentration routine. We decided to develop an effective concentration routine so that Drew would have plenty of mental energy for both his business and his family. An effective routine is based upon two key principles of mental energy.

First, picture concentration as a reservoir of energy. If the floodgates on the reservoir are wide open, this energy will empty quickly, causing you to burn out. To conserve these mental resources and perform at your best, the floodgates should open only for a short period and then close for a reaccumulation period. Drew had his gates wide open when he was managing his staff and making cold calls—two items that he mentioned took most of his good energy. By the end of the day, he had nothing left for his existing client base or his family.

Also, picture concentration as waves of mental energy. Just like waves in the ocean, your concentration will start slowly, gradually build, and then crescendo. To concentrate at the highest levels, you must allow your focus to build and then peak at the right moments. For Drew to be more successful, he needs to develop a concentration routine that allows his focus to peak for key tasks, that is, when he is working with his existing client base.

The following drills help you, as well as Drew, to manage your concentration more effectively.

DIAL IT IN

An effective concentration would take the analogy of a dial on these gates of our concentration reservoir. Picture a routine that lasts about one hour. In the first 10 to 15 minutes, the dial is set at 1. The gates are slightly open here. At this time, Drew should be executing easy tasks that require very little mental energy. For Drew, this might include managing an easy staff problem or making a warm call to a great client.

For you, it might be answering simple e-mails or other mindless must-be-done tasks. It may be critiquing a proposal that you wrote yesterday, just to fine-tune it a notch.

After about 15 minutes, the dial should be turned to 5. Here, the tasks will get harder and our focus will gain in intensity. For Drew, this could be dealing with more difficult management problems and making a few unfriendly cold calls. For you, this could include tasks that take a moderate amount of your mental energy. Perhaps, like Drew, it is making some key cold calls to some high-profile hopefuls, or tackling a problem you have been avoiding. This period should last for approximately 15 minutes.

Now, after about 30 minutes, the dial is cranked up to 10 and the gates of your concentration reservoir are wide open. Your mental energy is surging. At this time, Drew should engage in his most difficult tasks of the day, such as dealing with problem staff members or making key phone calls to important clients. For you, this time could consist of brainstorming new strategies for prospects, or writing a new proposal for that difficult client. This period should last about 15 minutes, and is the optimal amount of time for your focused energy.

The total time of the concentration routine is approximately 45 minutes. Following the completion of the last phase of the concentration routine, we should engage in a rethrottling period (described in the drill that follows). Once this re-throttling or reaccumulation period is over, we would start our concentration over again, beginning with tasks that take minor focus and moving to more energy-demanding tasks.

REACCUMULATION OF MENTAL ENERGY

Our mind works better when we follow a certain biological rhythm. We need to have waves of high intensity at work, followed by a re-throttling period. This re-throttling period should last for approximately 5 to 15 minutes and should be at the end of our concentration routine (as described in the previous drill). This period could consist of getting up from your desk and going to the bathroom, getting some water, talking to a colleague about nonwork topics, listening to the radio, or just meditating for a few minutes. This reaccumulation period allows us to remain fresh throughout the day as well as have mental energy left over for our family, keeping us happy and in balance in our lives.

CHAPTER THIRTY-FOUR

Flow with Your Concentration Style

We all have different concentration styles: a concentration style is how we focus our attention, process information, and react to our environment.

A great illustration of contrasting styles can be seen in the comparison of co-MVPs for the National Football League in 2003—Steve McNair and Peyton Manning.

Steve McNair's style is reminiscent of a matador. He reacts to the lineman as if they are charging bulls, weaving and jigging as he focuses on his receivers downfield.

While he makes plays from the pocket, it is obvious that his preferred style was to scramble and respond to the environment. McNair is in his flow when he is responding to the environment and adapting to an ever-changing play structure.

In contrast, Peyton Manning is more like a general commanding his forces. His preferred style is to stick with his plan and hold fort in the pocket even when 300-pound linemen are about to pounce on him. While Manning may scramble on some plays, his preferred concentration style is to stick with the plan rather than ad lib and make plays happen.

Although they have contrasting styles, both have been hugely successful, Steve taking the Titans to the Super Bowl and Manning winning the Super Bowl.

How do you react to pressure situations?

Are you like McNair? Or more like Peyton Manning?

Do you prefer to react to your environment or do you like sticking with your plan?

Being aware of your concentration style will help you perform better under the gun.

ARE YOU A STEVE MCNAIR?

Perhaps you have been trained to have everything planned during an important meeting or presentation. But developing a fine-tuned blueprint always felt confining and placed you into a noncreative box. Too much planning may stifle your excellence.

If your style is like Steve McNair's, you may feel most comfortable when you give yourself freedom of movement. While you may need some structure in your presentations or sales meetings, give yourself room to react and let your creative juices flow.

Follow Steve McNair's lead. Instead of connecting all the dots beforehand, you will find a flow when you react to the ever-changing situations at work.

ARE YOU A PEYTON MANNING?

Are you a planner like Manning? Do changing environments bother you? To be in your flow, do you need to have all your T's crossed and I's dotted before every meeting?

If Manning is your concentrative style, be well prepared for any and all situations at your next meeting. Plan your responses according to all of the reactions that you may get from your colleagues. With this type of preparation, you will be in your comfort zone when the pressure hits.

Knowing whether you are a McNair or a Manning will help you get to your own personal Super Bowl.

CHAPTER THIRTY-FIVE

Do the Twain

"Think outside the box."

We all have heard that cliché about thinking differently, thinking more creatively, thinking originally. And, if we can think outside the box, we may be able to move our career up a notch as well as make our boss look better and perhaps help company profits.

Unfortunately, we have been trained all along to perform by rote—to think inside the box and never break free. Throughout school, we simply regurgitated the information our teachers gave us, and got rewarded for such behavior. Thinking originally was never taught or encouraged. Now, when we are mandated to be creative and think differently, it is extremely difficult.

How can we think outside the box, when we have been mentally conditioned to stay inside the box?

Creative genius is not born, but formed with practice and hard work. Take the genius of Samuel Clemens, also known as Mark Twain.

One of the joys of visiting Hartford, Connecticut, is touring the Mark Twain House, which is a majestic craftsman's house, built near the end of the nineteenth century. Anyone looking at the house would know instantly that an original thinker lived within those four walls.

As in most tours, each room's unique feature is described. The docent points to all of the unique pieces of furniture and artwork acquired during Twain's worldwide speaking tours.

However, most apparent to Twain's magic is when you enter the "after dinner parlor." The docent points to a variety of interesting objects on the mantel above the fireplace and then explains a Twain family ritual. As his children sat in front of him, Twain would create a new story each night using the same objects. Some nights the pieces would involve a trek along the mighty Mississippi, while other nights featured princesses and dragons.

Yes, Twain was a creative genius, but he practiced his skill, every day and every night.

Dr. Win Wenger, author of *The Einstein Factor*, has written that creative genius comes from developing techniques that promote a different perception of our world. The following drills will help you write your own story, and hopefully get you to think outside the box on a regular basis.

THINK THE OPPOSITE

When Dick Fosbury began his high-jumping career in the early 1960s, the best in the world used the scissors technique to beat gravity. In this style of high jumping, the athlete leaps with his torso facing the bar in the horizontal position. He alternates each leg over the bar to create momentum, looking like a pair of scissors, snapping together and then opening again. Using this style of jumping, Fosbury could barely clear six feet, just average at that time for an amateur.

He transcended the sport when he thought outside the bar, however, and jumped opposite to the norm.

Fosbury developed a technique in which the head goes over first, with the back facing the bar in the horizontal position. The feet are the last to transcend the height. No one had ever gone over the bar with his back facing the bar. It was completely opposite to the then-current school of jumping.

The Fosbury flop, as it is now known, has since been discovered to work physiologically more effectively, transferring our energy over the bar at the key moments. Dick Fosbury used his ingenuity to create one of the most radical changes in the world of sport, jumping to a gold medal in the 1968 Olympics and becoming a legend in track and field.

Are you stuck in a creative rut? Want to jump ahead in your thinking? Perhaps you should try something totally opposite to what you are currently doing. Such an approach helped Fosbury leap to greatness.

DEVELOP CREATIVE ROUTINES

One of the most creative people of all time was William Shakespearc. While only a movie, *Shakespeare in Love* illustrates how the young Shakespeare tapped into his creative side. Before the young Shakespeare began to write, he would perform this ritual: spit on his hands, spin around twice, place his bottom on his stool, and then grab his quill and begin to write. This ritual indicated to his mind and body to start the creative process.

Create a routine to unleash your Shakespearean talent. It could be tapping on your desk twice with your favorite pen, or simply slapping your thigh three times. Do this routine before all your creative work as a method to tell your mind that you are about to move into the creative side of your brain. I would not recommend, however, that you spin around twice like the young Shakespeare—your colleagues may think you a bit eccentric.

TRY SOME DIALOGUE

Have you ever seen the movie, *What's Up, Tiger Lily?* Woody Allen took a Japanese movie and dubbed in an entirely new plot with dialogue that had nothing to do with the original movie. It was a creative masterpiece.

While most of us will never have the creative genius of a Woody Allen, we can take a valuable lesson from this movie.

Next time you are at home, turn on the television. Pick a show you have never seen and turn off the sound. Now make up some dialogue for the characters. Just go with it and be as creative as possible.

This drill will help you practice and harness your creative talent, for use in other areas of your business life. Perhaps you will get so good at it that you may want to write a few sitcoms.

EXERCISE YOUR CREATIVITY

Exercise promotes our creative energy. When we are exercising, our heart is pumping vital nutrients and oxygen to the brain. This supercharges our brain, promoting our ability to arrive at solutions and answers that may have seemed distant when sitting behind a desk. The next time you are stuck, go take a leisurely jog or a fast-paced walk. You will find that exercise is a magic pill that will stimulate your creative genius.

PART 5

EMOTIONAL DRIVE

To become a champion in any field, knowledge is not enough. Intention is not enough. To get results, action is essential. But action takes motivation, commitment, and high levels of energy.

Champions like Michael Phelps gain drive from their passion, while other winners such as Jie Zheng get supercharged from their pride. Winners know that the secret is in the dirt: Excellence comes from our hard labors. But the drive to excellence comes from more than just work—it also comes from giving ourselves to others. Champions like Kirk Douglas have discovered this principle through his generous deeds.

Are you passionate about your life? Are you committed to excellence? Do you put forth the effort needed to break through a plateau? Do you give as well as receive?

This section focuses on creating boundless energy and being committed to the cause of excellence. These chapters illustrate how to find passion and pride in ourselves, essentials to becoming a winner in life.

CHAPTER THIRTY-SIX

Passion Play—The Phelpsian Way

Almost 150 years ago, Henry David Thoreau wrote that we must live near the river from which our passion flows. When we find passion, we flow toward success.

Michael Phelps, the star of the 2008 Olympic Games in Beijing, China, found his flow at the swimming competition. Phelps did what no other Olympian had ever done before—win eight gold medals at a single Olympics.

Sports scientists have readily analyzed what makes Michael Phelps such a swimming phenom. Most have pointed to his physical prowess. He arm span is six feet, seven inches, and with it comes an incredible stroke. His trunk is longer than his legs, which allows him to float on the water more effectively. His ankles and knees are double-jointed, giving him incredible flexibility, which propels his body through the water like a dolphin. Perhaps, if we look even closer, we may find gills.

While his physical attributes, unquestionably, contributed to his Olympic records, one undeniable attribute stands out—his passion for swimming. Michael Phelps has stated that he loves to swim and that he feels more comfortable in the water than on land. If you look at the pictures of him at the Olympics, he is in pure ecstasy when competing. He is like a kid in a candy store, and that is what America loves about him. You can see the exhilaration in his face and his joy in every stroke.

Up to this point, Michael has said he will compete in the 2012 Olympic Games in London. What does he have left to prove? He will be richer than rich. It is estimated that he could make $100 million in endorsements. But to Michael, swimming is no longer about the money—it never was. It is not about proving his great skills—it never was. He will swim in London because he loves the pool.

When you do something because of passion, the pressure is greatly diminished. Ultimately, passion pushes the pressure out of the situation. Michael Phelps loves to swim and this will enable him to achieve greater speeds today and for years to come.

Linda Mason, founder and chairwoman of Bright Horizons Family Solutions, can empathize with Phelps. Linda said the best advice she ever received was when a colleague told her "Your passions do not have to be extracurricular. They can be central to your life. Unleash them, and you'll help other people unleash theirs."

When Linda and her future husband both graduated from the Yale School of Management in 1980, they postponed job offers at cushy consulting firms to run emergency programs in Cambodian refugee camps. They saw children left to die throughout the countryside. Linda, however, discovered that if you give food and basic medicine to young, malnourished babies who are ill, most will rebound.

After that prophetic mission, she decided to apply her passion back in the United States. She wanted to develop a company that would give children the best possible start in life—and this would be the core and mission of her start-up company. According to Linda, it was a slow, rugged start, and it was very difficult to get financial backing. But, by putting her passions first and then backing them up with financial numbers, she discovered that this philosophy gave her company a real business advantage. According to Linda, she witnessed tired-looking asset managers snap to attention when they felt her passion and caring for her project and the children. She eventually received the needed funding. Today, Bright Horizons has more than 600 child care and early education centers with every one passionate about the same cause, giving the children in their care a great start in life.

We all know passion. It is when you did what you loved because the activity created that inner spark—that feeling of exhilaration—of unabashed joy. It had nothing to do with money or praise. Unfortunately, as we go through life, it is hard for most to find that passion and even more difficult to find the passion for that job you have held for 10 years. But it is never too late to feel what Michael Phelps does when he enters the pool. The following drills will help you glide through every day more effectively and joyfully.

BE WITH THE ONE YOU LOVE

One of Stephen Stills's best-known lyrics is: "If you can't be with the one you love, honey, then love the one you're with." While these lyrics are timeless, I think Stephen would agree that we should try first to be with the one we love.

This is the imperative. If you do not have that Phelpsian feeling for your career or job, then change what you are doing—quit your job, find new work, go to school, try something new. Do what it takes to get into the Passion Zone.

When you find the Passion Zone, you never will want to stop what you are doing. Take Louis Armstrong's career. At age 69, Louis Armstrong's doctors told him he needed to stop playing jazz gigs and traveling. He was financially secure and unquestionably a musical legend. But Armstrong wanted no part of retirement. Satchmo, as he is lovingly known, believed his soul and spirit belonged to that horn. When you find your passion zone, you will never want to retire.

LOVE THE ONE YOU'RE WITH

The other option is often more realistic. Many are stuck in a current job or current career path that they can't just quit. You may have three kids and a mortgage. Leaving your job for a more passionate one is simply too risky. So, as Stephen told us, "Love the one you're with."

Focus on the aspects of your job that make you passionate. Reexamine your current situation to see if there are any opportunities to be passionate about—I am sure there are many. For example, you are an executive assistant who does the same mundane tasks over and over again. But you love people and love interacting with people. Then love every phone call—love the one you're with. Or, you are a manager for a beer distributor, and you have a passion for creativity, so focus on your creative spirit and develop new ideas to improve the product or distribution.

John Ruskin once wrote, "When love and skill work together, expect a masterpiece." Love the one you're with to create your own masterpiece at work.

CHAPTER THIRTY-SEVEN

Discover the Power of Pride

Jie Zheng was clearly outmatched and outgunned. Diminutive in stature, she was about to face the larger-than-life figure of Serena Williams in the 2008 Wimbledon semifinals. Although one of China's tennis stars, Zheng had only won three tournaments to date and was ranked in the top 30 in the world. Across the net was one of the greatest players of her generation. Serena Williams had been ranked Number One in the world and had won 18 Grand Slam titles at that point in her career. Most would predict that Zheng would get blown off the court.

However, Zheng had the power of pride on her side. A terrible earthquake had devastated her homeland just months before the tournament began. She pledged to donate all of her prize winnings to the earthquake victims in her country. Her pride was evident with every ground stroke, every step. Her energy on the court was amazing and so was her speed. Zheng matched Williams stroke for stroke, and at times, had clearly outplayed her on many points. Zheng was within one point of taking the match to a third set, but eventually lost 6–1, 7–6.

Anyone who saw the opening ceremony as well as the many competitions felt the power of pride exhibited by the Chinese athletes at the 2008 Olympic games. The Chinese athletes have given so much to those Games. Many of the athletes have lived and practiced at the Shi Cha Hai sports school, near the Forbidden City in Beijing. There, many of the students sleep four to six in a room and some see their parents just once a year. They generally work as many as seven hours a day on their games. One such Olympian, Ti Shen, who had been at the school for seven years was asked why she works so hard, to which she simply responded, "I am working for the pride of China."

Pride is one of the most powerful emotions. I felt its power when I completed my dissertation and defended it for the last time, in front of many critical committee members. I finally finished my long scholastic journey. I had obtained my doctorate in human performance and now I could teach at any university.

While I was relieved, what I remember most was the intense feeling of pride—it was quite euphoric—and that the feeling lasted for nearly six months. After that experience, I came to know the power of pride, and I can only wish every-one reading this book to have that same wonderful feeling. Following are drills to help you feel the power of pride as often as you can.

THE HARD MAKES YOU FEEL GREAT

Up until the 1980s, psychologists claimed that self-esteem was a product of rewards. It was recommended that educators give praise and many wonderful compliments to their students because it was thought that this would boost their self-esteem. Then the tide turned. Feeling good came not just from rewards, but was also a result of meeting challenges set forth by the teacher. When you overcome an obstacle with success, you feel a sense of accomplishment—a sense of pride—and that boosts your self-esteem.

In 2002, Alisa Camplin discovered a sense of accomplishment when she became the winner of the first gold medal for Australia in any Olympic winter sport. She won in freestyle skiing. But it was a very arduous road to reach the summit for Alisa.

In Australia, there are not many snow-capped slopes upon which to practice her sport. Instead, Alisa would ski down a mock shoot, do her twists and flips and land in extremely murky brown water. That was not the main difficulty, however. When she emerged from the water, Camplin would have many leeches stuck to her body. Clearly, Camplin suffered to achieve.

Most of us complain when the work gets too hard. But when the work is too easy, we do not appreciate what we have accomplished. In the movie *A League of Their Own*, Tom Hanks, who plays the manager of a woman's professional baseball team, epitomizes the importance of pride and sense of accomplishment when he shouts to his players, "The hard is what makes it great."

When the work is difficult, and yet you have risen to the occasion like Alisa Camplin, then, and only then, will you get the joy of feeling the sense of pride.

DISCOVER COMPANY PRIDE

Analogous to the Chinese athletes, when you have a greater sense of pride in your company, you will have greater energy and feel better about your efforts at work. To feel proud about your company's works, discover the following:

What does your company do to make you proud? Does it produce products that are safe or environmentally healthy?

What charities are your company affiliated with? You may know a few, but do you know all of them?

What charities or charitable deeds has the upper management contributed to?

What charitable acts have your colleagues participated in?

Pride will allow you to ace the competition!

CHAPTER THIRTY-EIGHT
The Secret Is in the Dirt

In the early 1950s, Ben Hogan began to dominate golf like no other player had ever done before. In 1953, he won the three majors he entered and won five out of the six events he competed in that year. He missed the PGA championships because of a scheduling conflict, and thus may have been the only player to have won the Grand Slam.

Ben was *the* man in golf. As such, everyone wanted to know his secret.

Was it his new grip? Some have mentioned that he rotated his grip a bit to the right to prevent his hook (or as Ben called it, "his terror of the field mice"). Some have mentioned that his weight shift had gotten better, while others have pointed to his shortened swing.

Ben would never reveal his full secret, but only allude to it. He would simply say, "The secret is in the dirt." Ben was notorious for beating balls before it was fashionable. Hogan said there were not enough hours in the day to practice everything needed to become a great player. Hogan learned that the only true secret in golf is hard work.

All the greats have the attitude that the road to excellence is paved with hard work. Bill Bradley takes it one step further. He believes that his excellence came from working harder than the next person. Bill Bradley has achieved the highest level of excellence in all he has done. He was a Rhodes scholar from Princeton, a former professional basketball star, and a United States senator. Bill said he learned this life lesson from one of his favorite coaches, who told him, "When you are not practicing, someone else is, and given equal ability, when you both meet, he will win."

Bill Bradley has written that his work ethic has carried over to many other areas of his life, from academics to politics. To this day, Bill still believes that no one can outwork him.

Most of us do not see the journey it takes to master an art, sport, or business—we see only the endpoint. The famous Vladimir Horowitz once said, "If I don't practice for one day, I will know it. If I don't practice for two days, my wife knows it. If I don't practice for three days, the world knows it." Every great success story has one facet in common— hard work.

DOUBLE IT

How much effort do you apply do your profession? To your career? Is it really enough, or are you just getting by? Are you just putting in half the effort that you need?

One time after both Gary Player and Ben Hogan had shot a 75 at the U.S. Open, Hogan said to Player, "You're going to be a great player. How much do you practice?" Player proceeded to explain what he did on the range and for how long. Hogan then stated, "Double it!"

The next time you are not succeeding at a task or in your career, ask yourself how much time did you really put forth to be successful. Be honest—did you pay the price?

Then tell yourself, "Double it!" Hogan would be proud of you.

CHAPTER THIRTY-NINE

Find Your Joy Spot

Casting for a television show is difficult, but casting the right ensemble for a brand new show can take it up a notch. Barbara Barna was given the most difficult task of putting together an ensemble cast for the TV show *Queer Eye for the Straight Guy*. Her charge was to have all five new members of the cast be both entertaining but also very knowledgeable in their respective fields.

The show's premise is that these five members (all of whom are gay) do a complete makeover on a straight guy. The show plays with the stereotypical notion that gay men have a way with style. Barbara Barna had to find a fab five: a fashion guru, a food and wine maven, a beauty expert, an interior decorator, and a culture guy. Plus, all of them had to get along and have great chemistry from the start. Barbara mentioned that it was one of the most stressful and difficult jobs she had ever faced. But more important, she had the most joy working on this show, and said that she did not feel any stress because of all the fun that the cast had with the show. As a result of great casting, *Queer Eye* won an Emmy and went on to become a huge hit for the Bravo network.

Barbara Barna fell upon the age-old wisdom that fun and stress do not mix. They are like oil and water. Pleasure in the action will help remove pressure from the day. Thousands of years ago, the Chinese philosopher Chuan Tzu knew this to be true when he wrote this proverb:

When an archer shoots for enjoyment, he has all the skill

When he shoots for a brass buckle, he gets nervous

When he shoots for a prize of gold, he begins to see two targets

Regardless of era, the greats know the importance of finding joy in a competitive situation. Willie Stargell, one of baseball's all time greats would say that umpires started the game by shouting, "Play ball!" They did not yell, "Work ball!" Willie loved to play baseball, but more important, he realized his level of play would be much higher if he was enjoying what he was doing. Dusty Baker, a great player for the Dodgers, felt the same. Dusty remarked that he would recall all the great times he had as a kid playing ball in his backyard and would bring all those pleasant thoughts to the plate with him.

More recently, Warren Sapp, of NFL fame as well as *Dancing with the Stars* fame, applied the joy principle as his mental advantage. As the sport psychology consultant for the TV show, I mentioned that Warren took the same mental philosophy from the gridiron to the dance floor. Warren realized that his joyful manner allowed him to let go of his self-doubt and negativity and perform at his highest level, whether it is the two-step or sidestepping an offensive lineman to sack a quarterback.

FINDING THE JOY AGAIN

Most people get so caught up at work with achieving a goal—attaining a quota, getting a prized client—that they forget the fun factor. In these difficult economic times, there is a huge concern with the monetary reward, and rightly so in many cases. It is vital to remember, however, why you gravitated toward your job. In most cases, there was a fun factor involved in deciding to take this career path.

You may not always be able to attain your goals daily, weekly, or monthly, but you can always commit to having fun. Davis Love Jr. said it best when he gave his son this timeless bit of wisdom for life: "Follow your dream and enjoy the trip."

ADD MORE LAUGHTER

Jimmy Demaret was one of the most colorful and amiable professionals to ever play golf. He was once known to say, "The Bible teaches an eye for an eye and a tooth for a tooth. I think that is a bit harsh. I believe in a joke for a joke." He won the Masters three times as well as many other tour events, intimating that a jovial attitude contributed to his great play.

Laughter brings us into a joyous state. Laughter, known as the universal elixir, can be one your best antidotes to a bad day at work. Researchers have found that laughter releases hormones such as endorphins. These hormones are considered the brain's natural opiates, giving you a sense of euphoria. In essence, laughing can make you feel good about a bad day.

Laughter will also increase your productivity at work. First, laughter places us in a good mood, and we tend to have more energy when our mood is lighthearted. Second, after a good laugh, our mental capacities increase such as our concentration levels and our ability to solve problems to difficult questions.

A good chuckle produces a relaxation response as well. When we laugh, our body does internal jogging: Our blood pressure surges, our heart rate increases, and we have greater muscle tension. Just like jogging with the feet, the body returns to normal physiological levels in a few moments after this activity. This rebound effect causes a relaxation response in our bodies.

You have a choice with laughter. When things go awry at work, you can get mad and throw a tirade. Or, you can choose to laugh at all those mishaps and difficulties at work and in your life. In this case, you will perform better with a relaxed and joyous feeling.

CHAPTER FORTY

Get a Mentor

The day had finally arrived. After 27 long years, Tommy Lasorda was offered the job as manager of the Los Angeles Dodgers. One of the first actions after learning of his new position was to walk into the office of General Manager Al Campanis, and give him a well-deserved hug.

Al had taken Tommy under his wing from the start and mentored him along the way to become the Dodgers' manager. First, Al made Tommy a scout to learn about the tools of talent detection. Also, Al made Tommy a minor league manager to learn about teaching younger players on both the mental and physical aspects of the game. Campanis also helped Lasorda become a coach on Walter Alston's staff (his predecessor) to learn about the other players in the National league. Al Campanis had given Lasorda all the guidance he needed to finally get his dream job.

From science to business to sports, people on top of their game usually had a mentor who helped them achieve their great success. Sir Isaac Newton once said that he could see farther by standing on the shoulders of giants. One of those shoulders belonged to Sir Edmund Halley, of comet fame. Halley challenged Newton to think through his original notions and to use mathematics and geometric figures to clarify his ideas. Furthermore, Halley not only encouraged Newton to write his famed work, *Mathematical Principles of Natural Philosophy*, but also edited and supervised the publication. Without Halley, Newton would be only a footnote in time and space.

Tiger Woods is also a giant in the game of golf, and he too stood on the shoulders of his good friend, Mark O'Meara. Mark took Tiger under his wing when he first came on to the tour. O'Meara gave advice on the many nuances of tour life, playing the role of big brother to the young upstart. O'Meara helped Tiger settle into the rigors of the PGA tour, and contributed to his development as a superstar.

Do you have a mentor?

In whatever field you are vying to achieve at the highest level, finding the right mentor is essential in developing your career. Here are a few suggestions for selecting a mentor.

DON'T FEEL GUILTY

Many people may feel guilty that they are taking a mentor's valuable time and energy. While that may be true to a point, mentors also benefit from the relationship. It is a win-win.

Billie Jean King has mentioned that she mentored many of the younger players of her generation, such as Chris Evert and Martina Navratilova. King taught the younger players how to interact with the media as well as how to deal with the pressures of being Number One in the world. But being a mentor helped Billie Jean in numerous ways, too. These younger players woke her up to new ideas, such as the belief that there should be higher standards as well as more money for women athletes.

Don't feel bad if you ask someone to be your mentor—she will benefit as much as you—maybe more.

CHANGE MENTORS

In his book about the development of talent, Gordon Bloom discovered that skill development follows a certain pattern. Most people are usually mentored by three different individuals. As the person progresses, they seek out a more experienced mentor.

In your case, work with a mentor for a given time (for example, six months) and you then may want to work with another one who can develop other skills that you may need in the future. For instance, you may want to work with a mentor who can develop your sales skills and another who may be able to develop your leadership skills, and another to help with your emotional intelligence skills.

MENTORING AS FRIENDSHIP BUILDING

Is there someone in your office with whom you just cannot connect, but believe it is important to have a better relationship? Do you want someone to appreciate you more?

Ask this person to be your mentor. Psychological research has shown that people like someone whom they have helped. Mentoring is all about helping, so it is a great tool to develop friendships as well as gain better knowledge.

MENTORS CAN APPEAR EVERYWHERE

Raymond Chandler is known as one of the great mystery writers of all time and wrote several movie screenplays, one being *The Big Sleep*, which starred Humphrey Bogart. In one of his earliest movies, Raymond was paired with an old-time writer from the silent era to complete a script. Raymond thought he was a young hotshot and had no desire to work with someone he deemed to be a has-been. The director had the pair each write their own version of a scene about the fall of a marriage. Chandler, who was a wordsmith, wrote great dialogue between the husband and wife, which intimated how their demise was imminent. The director thought the work was overkill—too many notes. He went instead with the scene written by the has-been, who wrote a simple scene of the couple in an elevator. The couple was dressed immaculately, with the husband wearing a fedora. A young attractive girl entered the elevator, to which the husband took off his hat. When she left the elevator on the next floor, he put his hat back on, indicating a clear rift in their relationship.

Chandler learned a great lesson about screenwriting from this has-been—show, don't tell.

CHAPTER FORTY-ONE

Drive to the Goal

In February 2007, Barack Obama declared his overarching goal to the world: He wanted to be the next president of the United States. He and his team devised a plan in which the primary goals of the campaign were to establish a grassroots approach as well as put the electoral process back into the hands of the people. The strategies to implement these goals were to have local political committees rather than statewide ones, as well as develop the Internet into a powerful political arm of the campaign. With the Internet, more people could spread Obama's message. Even better was that the Web became a great vehicle to raise unlimited funds for the campaign.

On November 4, 2008, the people agreed with his plan and strategies—Barack Obama was elected the president of the United States.

Marlo had an overarching goal as well—nothing as grandiose as high political office, but personally, it was just as important. As her New Year's resolution, Marlo set a goal of being a million-dollar producer in real estate for 2007. In the past, she had reached a half million dollars in sales, but never more. This goal would make her the first woman to reach the Million Dollar Club in Tucson, Arizona.

While this goal pumped her up initially and her effort increased, her results stagnated. Nothing had changed, except for her new and improved goal.

While overarching goals are essential to success in politics and business, they are not enough. Our future is not only determined by our goals, but our ability to make them real. Our goals become reality when we devise a plan to meet those objectives. More important, for this plan to work, it must have these essential components:

1. Short-term goals leading to the overarching goal
2. Strategies to reach those short-term goals
3. Assessment of whether or not the strategies are working
4. Reevaluation of the short-term goals

The following is an example of how Marlo created an effective goal setting plan, and more important, a template to reach your overarching goals in business and in life.

SHORT-TERM GOALS

As Taoism indicates, big things are accomplished by small steps. Short-term goals are the stepping stones to our overarching goal. To become a million-dollar producer, Marlo deduced she needed to meet more qualified buyers and sellers. Based upon her real estate experience, Marlo decided that a challenging short-term goal for every month would be to meet with at least five prospective clients. (She defined a prospective client as someone who was qualified to buy a piece of real estate or to sell a current piece of real estate.) Meeting with at least five prospective clients for Marlo meets the minimum criteria of good short-term goals. They should be specific, measurable, and attainable, but challenging.

STRATEGIES

The next key step in a goal-setting program is to develop effective strategies to reach your short-term goals. Marlo decided that she would join two new social networking groups, go to two new exercise groups (as a networking strategy) and increase her cold calls by 15 percent.

ASSESSMENT

While having strategies is key, we must also determine whether or not our strategies are effective. To accomplish this, we must evaluate our short-term goals.

After the first month, Marlo met only three qualified new clients, and after the second month, only two clients came to her attention.

REEVALUATION

The importance of assessment is the feedback we receive. Based upon Marlo's feedback, her strategies were not effective. Thus, to attain her overarching goal, Marlo would now need to change her strategies. She decided to stay with her new social networking groups because she felt they would bear fruit down the road, but she decided to give up on the cold calls. Marlo is very gregarious, and decided to use her charisma in a more productive way. She would conduct two real-estate seminars a month where she would give free advice about the market, how to get low-interest loans, and so forth. Marlo believed these seminars could be a gateway to meeting new qualified clients.

RE-START THE PROCESS

Marlo now has to reassess whether or not these strategies are helping her attain her short-term goals. If she does meet an average of five qualified prospective clients in the next few months, she should stick with her strategies. If not, she will need to develop new strategies, and start the process over.

Texas oil billionaire Bunker Hunt was once asked how to succeed. He said, "Find your dream, devise a plan, and then pay the price." While devising and implementing a plan takes lots of energy, the attainment of your goals is worth it.

CHAPTER FORTY-TWO

Commit to Finishing the Race

Derek Redmond epitomizes the spirit of determination. For Derek, the 1992 Olympic Games in Barcelona were to be his moment of triumph.

Redmond arrived at Barcelona with redemption on his mind. He was forced to withdraw from the 1988 Seoul Games because of an Achilles tendon injury. But in Barcelona, he was finally ready to race to his potential. His father, who accompanied him to the Olympics, as he did to all of his important races, knew something special was about to happen for Derek.

On the day of his competition, the Olympic stadium was packed. His first 400-meter race was the semifinal qualifying heat, with the top four finishers making it into the finals on the following day. As the gun went off, Redmond broke from the pack and took an early lead. With only 175 meters to the finish line, Redmond was a sure thing to make the finals. Suddenly, he felt his right hamstring snap and he fell onto the track.

As the medical crew arrived with a stretcher, Redmond told them, "No, there's no way I'm getting on that stretcher. I'm going to finish my race."

Then, in one of the most heart-warming Olympic moments ever, Redmond lifted himself to his feet, and hobbled down the track. At the same time, his father, Jim, hopped over the fence to race over to his son to assist him in his time of need.

The other runners had already finished, but to everyone's surprise and pleasure, the Redmonds were also going to finish the race—together. Arm in arm, father and son, 65,000 were applauding their every move. Through the searing pain, Derek Redmond heard the cheers, and said, "I wasn't doing it for the crowd. I wanted to finish the race. I'm the one who has to live with it."

Right before the finish line, Jim let go of his son and allowed Derek to cross the finish line by himself. Then Jim threw his arms around Derek again, with the crowd cheering their every move. The world of sports had just seen an Olympic moment of true greatness, in heart and spirit.

The scoreboard for the men's 400-meter semifinal race classified Derek Redmond's performance as "race abandoned." Derek's race was the opposite of abandoned. He was not to be denied his commitment to his sport or to his life—he was going to finish the race regardless of the pain or consequence. Following are some drills that can help you promote your commitment to excellence and to finish your race.

COMMIT TO THE FINISH

When Hank was on a business trip, he received the phone call that everyone dreads. His wife called him and said their house burnt down in a terrible fire. He first asked if the girls were okay, and she responded yes. He then asked if the pets were safe and again the answer was yes. His thoughts then became more pragmatic and shifted to the notion that he never finished his book. It was burnt in the fire. Sure he had backups, but they were all in the house—in ashes. All he could think was that if he had committed to finishing his book, he would have had it in his agent's hand, or a friend's hand to read it. But he never committed to finishing it, and now, the uncompleted manuscript had been destroyed in the fire. His lack of commitment to this important project led to its demise.

Sure, commitment takes energy, and perhaps Hank had other events that needed his energy. I am sure the same goes for you. There are many obstacles and hurdles that prevent you from finishing certain projects at work as well as in your life.

One solution to help you persevere through the hurdles is to develop a contract. An effective contract should include:

- How much time you will spend on this task each day or week. Hank could have listed 15 minutes each day he would spend on finishing his book.

- The benefits from finishing this task (such as getting a raise or promotion—or in Hank's case, a published book).

- A personal reward for finishing this task (taking that special trip abroad from the book royalties).

- Your signature and a colleague's signature. Simply by signing this contract, your level of commitment increases. You need to ask your colleague to remind you of your progress toward your goals as they relate to this contract.

- Post this contract somewhere so that you can gaze upon it daily. Hank could have had a picture of his favorite book on his refrigerator door to remind him of the importance of the project.

The great inventor Thomas Edison once stated that most successes are only one failure away. Today, Derek Redmond has a Nike commercial about his race in the 1992 Olympics. If Derek had given up, we would have never known his name, no commercial would have been made, and I would have never written about him in this book.

Commit to finishing. You never know what great events may happen to you.

CHAPTER FORTY-THREE

Rocket Past a Plateau

Most people are calling Zach Johnson the everyday man. He seems to be just like you and me, but he is not—he is the Rocketman. He has rocketed past most of his colleagues to the stratosphere on the PGA tour. He is in the rarified air of a major category.

Actually, Zach is unique because he has never reached a plateau—he keeps progressing. Zach was not the best player on his high school team yet he continued to improve and was good enough to play college golf. Clearly, his college, Drake University, is not a golf powerhouse, yet he continued to improve enough to play on the mini-tours. There, he honed his game enough to catapult himself onto the PGA tour. Still, he continued to improve and won a PGA tournament. Again, his skills did not remain stagnant and he again skyrocketed past most of colleagues to his first major win at the 2007 Masters.

The lesson we can gain from Zach's story is that we may never plateau in our skills. Unfortunately, most people (golfers and nongolfers) are not like Zach—we reach a certain level in our skills, in whatever venue, and usually stay there for a while or for an entire career.

Plateaus are inevitable on the learning trail. You will see vast improvement at first. Then, more likely than not, you will plateau for a period of time. After a while, you will see a little more improvement before you will plateau again. Sometimes plateaus can last for weeks, months, and even years.

Understanding why we have plateaus in the learning cycle can shed insight on how to break free. The learning cycle, with its ups and downs, has many parallels to the principles of muscle building. As an overall picture, the human body is an amazingly adaptive mechanism. When we lift weights, we force our muscles beyond normal levels, or, in other words, we stress out our muscles. (This process is called overloading the muscle.) As an adaptive response to counteract this overload, muscles produce more protein stimulating an increase in muscle fibers.

Our muscles will stop growing unless they are continually overloaded. That is, we will have plateaus in muscle growth if the force placed upon the muscles does not change. To experience muscle growth, you can add more weight to your routine, add more repetitions, or change your exercises. When you change these workout variables, your body is designed to respond with more muscle growth.

Just as muscles respond to overload, you can break through a plateau by adding stress to the system. Most people may think stress is bad—and it is when it becomes overwhelming. Getting out of a comfort zone, however, and pushing yourself to the limit can make you grow, both emotionally and mentally. This good stress, called eustress, forces us to adapt and extend ourselves past our current level of performance. Following are some suggestions to help you leap over the plateaus.

CHANGE SOMETHING

It is called a comfort zone for a reason. It is comfy, like a warm bed. Unfortunately, a journey engulfed by comfort and convenience is bound for no growth. To leap out of the status quo, or even skyrocket higher than you ever thought, you must continue to change. Even the greats must seek change to grow.

Bob Bowman, the coach of gold medal swimmer Michael Phelps, has said that they have a new plan for the 2012 Olympics. They are going to add a swim to his repertoire as well as change his training regimen. This is to ensure that Phelps will stay fresh and not lose his enthusiasm for the pool.

Change is stressful, and simple acts of change can be highly beneficial to keep us from going stale or stagnate, both mentally or emotionally.

What changes can you add to your business system?

Perhaps you could get an executive coach. If you do not have one, seek one out, get her advice and perhaps her help can bump you to the next level. If you already have a coach, and feel stale, it is time to get a new one.

Do you use the same scripted pitch for a cold call? Perhaps it is time for a rewrite. Do you use the same sales strategies that have been your calling card for the past 10 years? Maybe it is time to add some new techniques and tools.

Change something and you will rocket past that current plateau.

BE SMARTER WITH A LITTLE STRESS

For years, the belief was that our brain stopped growing when we reached the ripe old age of 18. We know now that is a myth. Our brain and its components will actually continue to grow throughout our life span. The key, though, is usage. We must continually use our brain for it to grow and expand. Performing challenging mental exercises such as writing and reading can stimulate our brains to continue to develop. But they all must follow the same principle. We must overload our brains with strenuous activities if we want to continue to be smarter.

What are you doing to grow smarter?

CHAPTER FORTY-FOUR

Catapult with Charity

In the movie *Spartacus*, Kirk Douglas helped to lead a slave revolt against Rome. While Kirk performed in 140 movies, this role was his defining moment. Spartacus catapulted him into legendary status on the silver screen.

Today, Kirk has led a revolt against the deplorable state of playgrounds in the Los Angeles area. More than 10 years ago, he and his wife saw a news story about the problems with the playgrounds and decided to make a difference. Kirk, always in consummate shape, knew that physical education contributed to a healthy mind and body.

Kirk started a foundation, largely financed by the sale of some of his art collection, which included works by Chagall and Picasso. The agreement with the Los Angeles Unified School District was to match the funds given by the Douglas Foundation, which usually gives $25,000 to each school. The foundation reached its goal with the opening of its 400th playground on May 29th, 2008. Kirk and his wife have attended every opening, with Kirk, at times, being the first to enjoy the ride down the new slide.

How can a guy who is 91 vibrate with such life, with such great energy? How can a guy who suffered a serious stroke still pulse with joy in each step?

According to Kirk, it is simple: The act of giving rewards him with an internal Academy Award. Kirk has mentioned that he gets so pumped by charitable acts and feels so good by this action that he thinks it is selfish. He loves to give and this action gives back to him in so many ways.

Do you give in your life? Do you do more than just donate funds? Do you perform acts of charity?

While you may not have the funds or time to start a foundation like Kirk has done, there are still many opportunities for you to give of your time and energy. Here are some reasons to act like Kirk.

BE GENEROUS FOR YOUR MENTAL HEALTH

Bob Hope once quipped, "If you haven't any charity in your heart, you have the worst kind of heart trouble." Whether being selfish can cause bad health is still open to discussion, there is no debate about great health resulting from giving. Dr. Karl Menninger has pointed out that one of the best ways to feel mentally and emotionally better is to help someone. He also claimed that generous people are rarely mentally ill. Developing a giving spirit helps to overcome feelings of deficiency in a positive way.

If you are feeling a little low, nervous, or just out of sorts, then go be generous. Do some charity work. Go volunteer for Habitat for Humanity. Do something that gives back. Giving away something of yourself will pay great dividends to your mental attitude.

GIVING INCREASES YOUR LIFE SPAN

Kirk Douglas may have figured out that giving does more than just give him great energy and make him feel great.

Giving increases his life span. Those who participate in charitable services live longer than those who do not. Perhaps community service gives us a substantial reason to keep on going—to keep on living. Catapult your life span with giving.

CHAPTER FORTY-FIVE

Leap Above Boredom

The date was Oct 21, 2008, and David Letterman had former President Bill Clinton on his show to discuss the upcoming election in a few weeks. David peppered the former president with questions, but most interestingly, he asked him, "Why would anyone want to take this job under these terrible conditions?"

At the time of the airing, the economy was in shambles: the stock market was plummeting every day, and we were in a recession that no one knew when it would bottom out. The war in Iraq was unresolved and there was a lack of confidence and a mistrust of politics and politicians.

Former President Clinton in all his glory responded with a very enlightening statement. He said he envied the incumbent president—yes, *envied* him. Clinton said how the new president can do so much for this country and that it would be such a great challenge and wonderful experience to turn our nation around.

President Clinton is a political champion with a winner's mentality. He has had low times in his political career, such as losing his first bid for reelection as governor of Arkansas. But he has always managed to rise again from his low points. President Clinton is the kind of person who seeks a challenge—one that tests his mettle. It is this trait, most likely, that propelled him to reach for and attain the pinnacle in his field.

B. C. Forbes once declared that golf without bunkers and hazards would be tame and monotonous. So would life. But our obstacles do much more than just make life more exciting. Dr. Mihaly Csikzentmihalyi, the foremost scientist in the field of human performance and development, has discovered the same ingredient that President Clinton clamors for—being in a challenging situation is one of the cornerstones for achieving flow (that is, having a peak performance). Regardless of the venue, from politics to sports, testing yourself is the secret to getting into the Zone. Without the hazards on the golf course or in our life, we could not reach our highest performance state.

The greats may know this principle intuitively and create situations filled with challenges to play at their best. Michael Jordan, one of the greatest basketball player of all time, has stated that he tricks himself into a challenging mode. Jordan indicated that even when he was on top of his game, he would declare a weakness that he needed to work on and develop. He wanted to add continual challenges into his already great game.

Seeking challenges also promotes our authentic happiness. Famed football coach Jimmy Johnson would tell his team the meaning of true happiness is being involved in a challenge. Johnson would explain that he could gain pleasure from eating a good meal, but that pleasure doesn't equate to happiness. "To be happy," Johnson says, "I've got to be challenged; I've got to accomplish things; I've got to have some sense of satisfaction and achievement." Johnson knew that all champions seek challenges to overcome because doing so is the mark of true happiness.

LEAP ABOVE YOUR BOREDOM

On the flip side of flow is boredom. According to Dr. Csikzentmihalyi, boredom is caused by a lack of challenge. You cannot achieve flow without being appropriately challenged. No one ever found flow when applying screws to a widget.

Are you feeling flat in your job and life? Have you lost your challenge mentality? Are you simply going through the motions? Are you progressing toward burnout? Your answers are probably yes if you have being doing the same job for the past decade without any real change in tasks. Regardless of the difficulty of one's job, we can still be bored and flat if we are not continually adding challenges to the mix.

To accomplish this, ask the following questions:

What can I add to challenge me at work?

How can I find more stimulation at my current job?

Can I increase my quota to be more challenging?

Can I add more seminars to my schedule?

Can I change my current situation, such as become a manager or more of a leader?

To leap above boredom—to be like Michael Jordan—make it your mission to add challenges to your job.

PART 6

EMOTIONAL BALANCE

Real champions make a difference, in every venue. Tiger Woods leads a life that has meaning off the golf course. Balance also comes from acceptance. Champions like Annika Sorenstam and Paul McCartney let go of factors outside of their control when events do not go as planned. Winners such as Venus Williams have balanced their life's portfolio with many wonderful activities. Champions value more than just winning, but prize their integrity and honor.

Do you have a life full of balance and perspective? Do you accept the bad with the good? Do you value integrity in all your decisions?

This section shows how to find serenity in a chaotic world.

CHAPTER FORTY-SIX

Discover Your Inner Tiger (Woods)

Are you happy?

Not just this moment as you read this sentence, but in your life, in what you do?

Being happy is your right.

More than 200 years ago, Thomas Jefferson penned in the Declaration of Independence, "We hold these truths to be self-evident, that all men are created equal, that they are endowed by their Creator with certain unalienable rights, that among these are Life, Liberty and the pursuit of Happiness." Our founding fathers thought that our right to happiness ranked as important as our right to be free from tyranny.

Unfortunately, throughout the years, this pursuit has been commonly misunderstood. One myth is that leisure brings happiness. Taking a vacation or going to a good movie can make us feel better for a while, but that kind of happiness is fleeting. So we repeat these activities or replace them with others that don't bring lasting happiness, either. It is as if our happiness bucket has holes and we have to continually fill it to find joy in life.

Success may not plug up our happiness bucket either. In a recent interview on the CBS news show *60 Minutes*, New England Patriots quarterback Tom Brady said that while he has won three Super Bowls and has achieved his wildest dreams, he still feels empty. On the show, Brady mentioned that he ponders, "Is this all there is?" He believes there must be more.

Why can't success fill up our happiness bucket?

True happiness is a verb. Happiness involves engaging in meaningful endeavors that inspire us from the heart. Martin Seligman, author of *Authentic Happiness*, declares that long-lasting happiness stems from the ongoing dynamic performance of worthy deeds. Authentic happiness is the deeply felt sense that your life is full, whole, and complete. Meaning in your life fulfills you. It brings long-term happiness.

With a smile that can light up your entire television set, Tiger Woods epitomizes authentic happiness. Yes, he is living his dream by playing professional golf as a career, and yes, Tiger is having a fantastic career.

But Tiger is much more than just a golfer. He has said, "Golf is what I do, not who I am." Tiger is a citizen of the world. When he became a professional, he started the Tiger Woods Foundation, which helps underprivileged youths throughout the world. The foundation recently opened a school in Los Angeles where children learn about art, physics, video construction, and, of course, golf.

Tiger Woods lives a life of meaning. This meaning gives him inspiration to do more, to achieve higher, to be a better person. In *Training a Tiger*, Earl Woods wrote that one of his son's greatest weapons on the course is the target of his inspiration—he plays for his foundation and all those kids involved in his programs. Tiger knows golf is a vehicle to make a difference and this meaningful purpose inspires him through the pressure.

Joseph Campbell, author and philosopher, argued that while we search for the meaning of life, we desperately seek the meaning in our lives. We seek inspiration everyday at work and our ability to find meaning can help us tap into inner strengths and resources we did not know existed.

The following drills can add energy to your days by adding meaningfulness to the workplace.

MAKE A TIGER LIST

Will Steih, a retirement consultant, came to me feeling unhappy and uninspired about his work and life. When this occurs, I have my clients develop their own "Tiger List." I had Will create a list of all the meaningful contributions his job has made to himself, his family, the community, and the world in general. In Will's case, one item on his Tiger List was how he helped put one of his client's son through college. The son is now at Vanderbilt Medical School helping to discover a vaccine for breast cancer. I suggested to Will to remember this grand deed any time he feels a bit low in his life.

Like Will, you can make your own Tiger List. Ask yourself the following questions:

1. How has your job made a meaningful contribution to your company?
2. How has your job made a meaningful contribution to the community? To society in general?
3. How does your job make a meaningful contribution to you? To your family?

Once you have your Tiger List, post it on your computer or somewhere in your office. When you find yourself a bit down in the dumps or just stressed, take a glance at your Tiger List. It may not cause you to give a fist pump, as Tiger Woods does after a great putt, but reminding yourself of what's on it should give you a jolt of needed motivation.

LEAVING A LEGACY

We still do not know what Tiger's legacy will ultimately be, both off and on the course. Acknowledging that you have a legacy is recognizing your purpose. We all have the ability to create some type of change—to influence many lives in a positive way—as a role model or giving your time to a charity or perhaps creating your own charitable fund.

What is your legacy? What do you want it to be?

Write a legacy statement.

As George Bernard Shaw once declared, "There is much joy when we know our work has a mighty purpose."

CHAPTER FORTY-SEVEN
Let It Be

We all have highs and lows in daily life, all of us, even Paul McCartney. While McCartney had many career highs, much of 1968 wasn't one of them. The Beatles' career was winding down and the break-up was looming. Single at the time, he was staying up too late, drinking, clubbing, and, as he put it, "wasting his life away."

Paul also mentioned that at this time in his life, he was depressed and not feeling too good about himself. Comfort came one night for him, however, during a dream he had about his mother, Mary. She died when he was only 14 and he could barely remember her face. But in this dream, her face appeared crystal clear, particularly her eyes. She said only three words to him in a gentle, reassuring voice, "Let it be."

McCartney awoke with a great feeling. He felt his mother had given him a message he desperately needed—it would all work out, and that he should just go with the flow.

Soon after waking, he went to the piano and started writing the now-famous lyrics, "When I find myself in times of trouble, Mother Mary comes to me, Speaking words of wisdom, Let it be."

"Let it Be" became McCartney's anthem and it's one of the songs he is best remembered for with the Beatles. As he described it, writing the song felt like magic.

Applying the philosophy behind "Let it Be" to the business world can help us learn to accept the inevitable downturns in life. When they occur, and they will, some salespeople lose their resolve. Others panic or begin to doubt themselves or even lose faith in their abilities. In the most extreme cases, what started as a slide can turn into a nasty slump.

We have to accept the times when we are struggling and learn to just go with the flow—just let it be—like Michael Jordan did regularly on this way to becoming one of the greatest basketball players of all time.

Adopting a mindset similar to the one Jordan had during his playing days can help a salesperson learn to accept and move past a sudden downward slide.

Jordan went with the flow because, beyond being a great basketball player, he understood statistics. He knew that at certain times during a game, he would miss some shots in a row. But Jordan always kept shooting because he knew a hot streak was just around the corner.

It's basic math. Say Jordan was averaging 50 percent from the field. That didn't indicate that he was hitting one and then missing one, but rather, he would experience a different sequence of hits and misses.

One sequence might have been two misses followed by six baskets followed by eight misses followed by four baskets. The possible variations are limitless.

Whether he was hitting or not, Jordan knew that by the end of the game, he would probably end up making half his shots. He wouldn't let the misses disturb him.

Here is a tip to help you think more like Mike and Paul and just let it be.

BE A SALES STATISTICIAN

Figure out your percentage related to your sales performance. For instance, let's say you average 14 face-to-face interactions for every 50 cold calls you make. You believe a face-to-face interaction is key to making that sale. Your face-to-face average in this case is 28 percent.

Next, create a random pattern of hits and misses that reflect your percentage with "X" equaling hits or "Face-to-Face interactions" and "0" equaling misses—no interactions. Your sequence might look like this:

0000XXXXX0000X000XX0000000000X000X000
X000X000X00X0

After analyzing your sequence, you might learn that, on occasion, you may make 10 calls without scoring a face-to-face interaction. Don't look at those periods in your days or your weeks as chances to second-guess your talents, lose your composure, or doubt your abilities. Realize that you'll get hot again and that better times are right around the corner. Place such a sequence on your computer to remind you of McCartney's words. Sometimes it's important to just let it be.

CHAPTER FORTY-EIGHT
Serenity Now

God, give us grace to accept with serenity the things that cannot be changed, courage to change the things that should be changed, and the wisdom to distinguish the one from the other.

The Serenity Prayer, by Reinhold Niebuhr

Annika Sorenstam has become an internationally recognized sports superstar. She attained this status when she mustered up the courage to compete against the men on the PGA tour.

For weeks building up to the event, she made numerous appearances on a variety of television shows, from David Letterman to the Today Show. Everyone wanted to know why she was competing and whether she would play on the men's tour as a permanent fixture.

During the week of the event in Fort Worth, the eyes of the world fell upon her. News media came from every part of the world. Her press conferences took hours to complete. Reporters bombarded her with questions from thoughts about the course to whether she believed she could make the cut. The world wanted to know the mind of Annika.

The pressure was immense, to say the least. Annika mentioned that the pressure was analogous to all four majors rolled into this one tournament.

But true to form, Annika applied her great mental game to this incredible moment. She focused on the controllables, in her golf and in her life. Annika disregards what is beyond her control and has stated that once the ball leaves her clubface, she ceases to worry about it. She cannot control whether the ball will take a bad bounce or good one, so she removes that concern from her mind.

Annika played amazingly, outscoring 18 men. While she still missed the cut, something magical did happen for Annika and the game of golf that week.

Teresa Shiping used the same philosophy as Annika when a shakeup came to the financial world in the last decade. From 1994 to 1998, Teresa worked for companies that went through five different mergers. But each time, she didn't worry about who would be her new boss or whether she would like this person or vice versa. All Teresa did was focus on what she could control—her hard work, good networking, preparation, and great time management. According to Teresa, focusing on factors within her control allowed her to manage her emotions most effectively—to be resilient to change, to stay positive, and to withstand all the pressures. In turn, she believes her great attitude about her controllables allowed her to transcend to the top of her game. Today, Teresa stands tall, being one of the senior vice presidents at a top asset management firm.

In actuality, Annika and Teresa became champions in their field because they both used a form of the Serenity Prayer to achieve their wonderful success. As this prayer dictates, when you can accept any outcome, and let go of factors beyond your control, you will find serenity in your life. Annika and Theresa used this philosophy to alleviate some of the incredible pressure and gained the great respect and admiration due them in their respective fields.

William James, a foremost psychologist at the turn of the twentieth century, remarked that the art of being wise is the art of knowing what to overlook. The following drills can help you become wise about finding your serenity.

FIND YOUR SERENITY

Let the Serenity Prayer be your advantage at work. Finding serenity at the workplace involves a three-step process. First, you must gain the wisdom to recognize the difference between those factors in your business life over which you have control and those factors in which you have limited influence. To accomplish this, list the top ten worries you have at work (see the following worksheet, Step 1). These worries can include such items as what other co-workers think about you, what may happen to your company (such as a merger), whether there will be layoffs, and the economy. Next, place the worries into two categorical boxes: Can Control and Cannot Control (see worksheet, Step 2).

With the worries you placed into the Cannot Control box, be like Annika and find the mental strength to accept those factors over which you have limited or no control. These factors are outside any influence you have, so just let them be.

If you find yourself continually thinking about these uncontrollables, use this psychological tool. Write these worries on a piece of paper. Then crumple up the paper and throw it into a trash can. When you start thinking about those problems, say to yourself, "trash can." Do this every time you begin to think these unproductive thoughts. You will eventually be able to throw away all of your uncontrollable worries.

Now here comes the courage part. With the worries you placed into your Can Control box, devise one strategy for each of those worries (see worksheet, Step 3). For instance, you worry about getting a raise. While you cannot control whether the boss will actually give you more compensation for your hard work, you can control facets contributing to a raise. For instance, you could have a strategy that you will take on extra work, work late if necessary, and make sure your work exhibits the highest quality. Following a specified strategy will not only help you achieve desired goals, it will also give you a greater sense of control over the situation, ultimately reducing your anxiety.

When you learn to let go of factors you cannot control and focus only upon those factors that really are within your control, you will discover your serenity at work.

SERENITY PRAYER WORKSHEET

Step 1: Create a Worry List

1.
2.
3.
4.
5.
6.
7.
8.
9.
10.

Step 2: Place Worries into Either a Cannot Control Box or Can Control Box

Cannot Control	Can Control

Step 3: Develop Strategies for Can Control Worries

1. Can Control worry: —————————————
   Strategy: ———————————————
2. Can Control worry: —————————————
   Strategy: ———————————————
3. Can Control worry: —————————————
   Strategy: ———————————————
4. Can Control worry:
   Strategy: ———————————————
5. Can Control worry: —————————————
   Strategy: ———————————————

CHAPTER FORTY-NINE

The Best Are Never Satisfied

To Mark Moore, his true paycheck did not come from his hard labors, but rather from all the interactions and compliments he would get from past employees he had mentored. Along the way in his career, Mark had mentored hundreds of people in the world of financial advising to be happier in their lives and more effective at their jobs. To this day, many still call him for his advice, even though Mark is no longer their boss. Such compliments extend far beyond any monetary reward.

Mark Moore would mentor many of his colleagues following the principle of "The Triple A": Activity, Accountability, and Advancement. Activity implies focusing upon effective actions to reach your goals. Accountability refers to being responsible for your actions but also to be accountable to having balance in your life. These two A's flow into the third: Advancement of learning. Mark promotes the idea that to be the best you can be in any field, you must actively pursue knowledge, not only in your field but outside of your field as well. You will then have greater balance in your life and be more likely to reach your goals.

According to Mark, this process of advancement of learning is not just a principle for being the best in business, but in all endeavors. This is so true. Just look at the best performers in the field of sport.

Mia Hamm was always on the path of being the best through her advancement of learning. In college, Mia Hamm walked into her coach's office, Anson Dorrance, and announced that her goal that year was to be the best woman collegiate soccer player. She asked what she had to do to reach that lofty goal. Dorrance told her that striving to be the best was a decision she had to make every day—she had to choose between being mediocre and being excellent every time she woke up. Mia Hamm realized that being the best is like flipping a light switch: it is not glamorous, it is not about glory, and it is not a God-given talent. It is about a commitment to learning, to progressing, to being the best. It is about believing that good is not good enough.

Tiger Woods also lives by this philosophy. Although he won his first major, the 1997 Masters by 12 strokes, he was not satisfied with his swing mechanics. Tiger believed that his swing was too long and his clubface was too shut at the top. He could not hit the soft flowing shots he would need to win the other majors. As a result, he and his swing coach at that time, Butch Harmon, went to work and revamped his swing. Tiger's attitude of never being satisfied has allowed him to be the youngest winner of all the majors. In fact, Tiger is the first golfer to ever win four major titles in succession. Even today, with all of his great achievements, he is continually striving to be better and better.

When we become complacent with our abilities, we stop growing and achieving. There is an old African parable that describes how we all must keep progressing in our lives:

Every morning in Africa, the gazelle wakes up and knows it must run faster than the fastest lion.

Every morning, a lion wakes up and knows it must out-run the slowest gazelle or it will starve.

It does not matter whether you are a gazelle or a lion; when the sun comes up, you better start running.

The following advice will help you to run toward your greatness.

TAKE TIME TO READ

The wisdom captured in books is immense and immeasurable. Authors are unique people. They want to share with you all their knowledge and good tidings.

Bill Gates knows this to be true. He has mentioned that he makes time for reading each night, and it is much more than just topics like computers or economic forecasts. Rather, he reads outside his comfort zone and has wisely stated, "If I were to read only what intrigues me, I would be the same person I was when I started, so I read it all."

Be better than yesterday—read it all.

DEVELOP NEW TOOLS TO YOUR TRADE

Nobel Laureate Albert Szent-Georgyi said that the basic human instinct is to evolve, to keep progressing to the next level. Earvin Johnson Jr. had great basketball instincts, which led to his wonderful nickname, "Magic." But his true instinct was his acceptance and willingness to develop new tools to be the best in the game. Magic spent one summer learning how to shoot a sky hook. He became famous for this magical shot. Nonetheless, Magic retorted that his greatness lay not in shooting hook shots but rather, "It's wanting to learn something new. I want to constantly be adding new tricks to my game."

Are you willing to add new tricks to your trade? If so, what are some new tools you can add to your repertoire? Can you add more advanced computer skills? Better writing skills? Greater speaking skills? Better negotiation skills?

ALWAYS ASK WHY

Ted Williams, known as the greatest natural baseball hitter of all time, always focused his attention on swinging the lumber. Ted Williams wanted to know as much as he could about hitting. Figuratively, he wanted to get a Ph.D. in the science of hitting. In his autobiography, *My Turn at Bat*, Williams wrote, "I want to know why. I think *why* is a wonderful word."

Why not fall in love with the question *why?* If it worked for one of the greatest hitters of all time, I am sure it can help your game, in business and life.

Ask yourself five whys each day at work.

Why did my boss give me that feedback? Why did this proposal not work? Why were my clients not as engaged as they should be? Why am I not reaching my goals? Why am I not motivated?

The whys will lead to the answers of your success.

PEACE OF MIND

When Socrates was in prison facing death, his jailers mocked him and asked, "Why do you not prepare yourself for death?" Socrates replied, "I have prepared for death all my life by the life I have lived."

Vying to be better every day will give you peace of mind—every day you live.

CHAPTER FIFTY

Let Integrity Flow

Grit is an integral part of the word *integrity* for a reason. John Wooden has written that sport does not build character, but rather, sport reveals character. Our integrity shines under *gritty* conditions. Our character will shine when the pressure is on and adversity is knocking upon our door.

Integrity knocked on John Wooden's door and he answered. In the late 1940s, the young John Wooden was looking for his first basketball coaching job. He had preferred to work at the University of Minnesota, a very prestigious basketball school at the time, and John was one of the top prospects for that job. A young school, however, UCLA, had offered him a job as head coach. Wooden could not keep UCLA waiting, so he gave Minnesota a deadline. The date had passed, and so true to his word, Wooden signed with UCLA.

Minnesota had wanted to make the call before the deadline, but it turned out that a snowstorm had knocked out the phone lines. This was an acceptable excuse to go back against his promise to UCLA and take the more prestigious job. But Wooden saw beyond what his immediate desires were at that time. He was true to his word and the rest is history—Wooden became a legend as a coach and mentor to thousands of young men at UCLA over his career.

Standing by your integrity and sticking to your word goes far beyond the hardwood. It helped make Southwest a dominant force in the airline business. Herb Kelleher, chairman and former chief executive of Southwest Airlines is a man of his word. Kelleher believes you build trust with integrity, by keeping promises, and sticking to commitments. He further believes that when people know they can count on you, they will work hard for you.

Kelleher is not just talk; he also backs up his words with actions. When the company was just getting off the ground, he had to negotiate the pilots' contracts—and it was not a favorable one for the pilots. But to show his commitment and integrity, Kelleher said he would freeze his own pay for the same five years that the pay of the pilots would be frozen in those early years. By holding true to his integrity, Southwest has taken off.

Integrity will find you out. When you have integrity, people will work as hard as they can for you, as they have for John Wooden and for Herb Kelleher. When you lack integrity, people will find out, and you may be forever tarnished, in sport as well as in business.

In the 2006 World Series, many of the players for the St. Louis Cardinals suspected the opposing pitcher, Kenny Rogers, of violating a major rule—the use of pine tar on the ball. Using pine tar would give Kenny more control over his pitches and more control over the game, but it is illegal. Only suggested, never proven, Rogers denied the allegations and said he used only dirt and rosin to muddy up the ball. But the sports media and players alike believe he may have crossed the line to get a win. The dirt on the ball may have sullied his reputation forever.

Crossing the line has been commonplace in business. Look at Enron, where corporate leaders bilked millions of dollars from their own employees. Jeff Skilling, the CEO at

Enron, expressed remorse when he was found guilty but still believes he did nothing wrong. Jeff Skilling will be forever tarred by this debacle, disregarding any good deeds he may have done in his life.

According to Billie Jean King, a woman of honor as well as a champion tennis player, integrity is probably the most important quality one can have to maintain peace of mind. King further adds that when we act and live within our ethical system, we will not only find true success but also serenity.

If this is true, then why do so many people disregard its power, its potency in our lives?

That is the million-dollar question—but beyond the scope of this book. Rather, the conclusion of this chapter focuses on how we can better capture our integrity.

LET INTEGRITY BE YOUR ULTIMATE FRIEND

Abraham Lincoln once said the following about his integrity, "I desire to conduct the affairs of this administration that if, at the end, when I come to lay down the reins of power, I have lost every other friend on earth, I shall have at least one friend left—and that friend shall be down inside me."

Integrity must be your ultimate friend for you to make the most ethical decisions. As Lincoln discovered, when he followed that friendship, he knew he had made the best decision.

INTEGRITY MUST FLOW ACROSS ALL SITUATIONS

We must see possessing integrity as an all-or-nothing principle. Arthur Gordon, a politician and author, said it best when he described integrity analogous to that of a principle in mathematics: An integer is a number that isn't divided into fractions. Just so, a man of integrity isn't divided against himself.

A person of true integrity has integrity in all situations. You cannot have integrity in your social relationships, but not in the office. You cannot bend the truth with one client and not want to bend other truths with other people. You cannot cheat on the golf course and then have the utmost integrity with your family.

Integrity flows from one aspect of our lives to all others. If we act without honor in one aspect, it will be easier to act dishonestly in other areas of our life. Have honor in all you do, and your life will flow with integrity.

BE AWARE: HAVING INTEGRITY MAY COST YOU

J.P. Hayes had already won on the PGA tour and accumulated more than $7,000,000 in earnings. Unfortunately, however, he lost his card for the 2009 season. When that happens, even the best players in the world must go back to the grueling qualifying tournament, known as "Q" school. Hayes was set to finish in the top 20 and advance to the third round of Q school. He was in a great position to head back to the PGA tour, but then his integrity got the best of him.

J.P. discovered that he was playing with a prototype Titleist ball that got accidentally pulled out by his caddy and thrown into play. J.P. knew it did not conform to the rules of the game. No one else could have known he was playing with an illegal ball, but J.P knew and so he called the infraction on himself. He was subsequently disqualified.

Playing with your integrity may cost you in the short run, but in the long run, you will always be a champion like J.P. Hayes.

CHAPTER FIFTY-ONE

Temper Competitiveness with Mastery

Pete Sampras, the greatest tennis player of his generation and winner of 18 majors, never won a national junior singles title. As a junior, Pete had played up, competing against players at higher levels and in older age groups, to get more competitive experience. Winning was not as important to him. Rather, developing his skills was his ultimate focus. Ironically, Pete Sampras made it to the top because he did not focus on winning, but rather upon the process of getting better.

The problem with a focus on winning is that it can lead to an increase in our feelings of pressure. Football coach Jimmy Johnson also got ironic with his players when he would give a pep talk about the perils of winning as the only objective. To illustrate this point, Johnson would tell his players that construction workers have to cross beams that are 1,000 feet in the air to get from one site to the next. If they focus on falling (the outcome), the pressure would be enormous. They would probably fail—or fall, in this case. To reduce their pressure, the construction workers have to focus on the process—one step at a time—to get across the beam. Ultimately, to Jimmy Johnson, the focus should be on the steps to winning.

Sports research has supported the difficulties with a focus primarily on winning and outcome objectives. Athletes who focused only upon winning had less enjoyment, lower performance, and a greater probability of dropping out of the sport. In direct contrast, athletes who focused on the process of getting better, like Pete Sampras, had a decrease in anxiety, yet an increase in confidence and performance. A focus on mastery led to an increase in longevity in the activity as well.

It is true that when the focus is all about winning and losing, the pressure can be enormous. At times, competition can feel like a mountain fighting against us, and in many cases, the mountain will win.

But let's be realistic—the competitive world of business is all about winning. Outcomes are magnified. People in business, regardless of profession, are evaluated on a continual basis. This evaluation is usually based on a social comparison—if you are not as good as your colleagues, then you may lose out on a promotion, or worse, get fired. If you are in the business world, you cannot disregard outcomes and being the best at your job.

In fact, a focus on being the best can be quite motivational. Many great performers use social comparison as a tool to boost energy. Trying to be the best salesman, accountant, lawyer, or manager can stoke the fire that drives those many hours to master specific skills that will help get you to the top. Without that competitive fire, many lose their desire.

Given that a focus on being the best is vital to business, then the question of interest should be: When should competitive objectives be emphasized? When should winning and being the best be a top priority? How can we use competitive objectives as an advantage to our success?

I believe Nick Faldo has the answers to these important questions.

COMBINE COMPETITIVE AND MASTERY OBJECTIVES

In the mid-1980s, Nick Faldo was one of the best golfers in Europe. However, he wanted to be one of the best golfers in the world. To accomplish this, a golfer must win major tournaments. Unfortunately for Nick, his swing would not hold up under the pressure. As fortune would have it, Nick connected with David Ledbetter, who rebuilt Nick's swing piece by piece.

This was not an easy path and his swing took many years to revamp, and as such, his ranking plummeted. During this period, Nick was willing to downplay his competitive objectives of being the best and focus primarily upon mastering his new swing.

Ultimately, all the hard work paid off. In 1989, he won his first Masters, a golfing major, and since has won two more Masters titles and three British Open titles. Nick was recently voted into the World Golf Hall of Fame. By emphasizing both competitive and mastery objectives, Nick became an all-time great.

My research supports Nick's journey to glory. The best way to reach the top of your game is to possess both mastery and competitive goals. I discovered that those individuals who had both goals exhibited the greatest persistence, the most joy, and the highest level of performance in the task. Like Nick, the best performers tempered their competitive fire with mastery objectives.

The issue should not be whether a mastery or competitive goal is more conducive to success. The issue, rather, is timing. That is, both objectives can feed off each other so as to attain the highest level of achievement. The key to success is to exhibit each at the most appropriate time.

To accomplish this, have goals that pertain to certain competitive outcomes such as quotas and benchmarks to meet. But sprinkle mastery goals into the formula as well. For example, if you are a pharmaceutical sales rep, have challenging high level quotas to boost your motivation. But also have some mastery objectives, such as becoming a better communicator, a better negotiator, or a better closer. Focus on improving key skills in your career as well as the attainment of specific performance benchmarks.

Here is the rub: When sales are good and you are meeting your quotas, you will feel good about yourself. However, if the economy gets bad or your sales go into a lull, you can still feel good if you believe you are getting better at some of these key skills. You know that if you master the skills of being a great communicator and negotiator, then your sales will eventually improve. Having balance across both competitive and mastery goals will make you feel great on a variety of fronts.

CHAPTER FIFTY-TWO

Diversify Your Life's Portfolio

A balanced life gives you perspective and comfort. Venus Williams, the former Number One women's tennis player, has a full plate of balance. During a television interview at the 2003 U.S. Open, the commentator asked Venus how she felt about her injury withdrawal from the tournament. With a glow reserved only for enlightened individuals, Venus mentioned that she felt disappointed, yet eternally happy. Venus then spoke with joy about her new interior design company and her new tennis clothing line. Venus Williams is much more than just one of the greatest tennis players of all time.

Donald Trump has diversified his work portfolio. While he started as a real estate investor, most know that Donald has branched out his brand. He is the author of a few best-selling books, a host and contributor to a top-ranked television show, a golf course builder, and is involved in a variety of other business ventures. While some of Trump's critics would say that much of these activities feed his ego as well as his brand, all of these endeavors add to his balance and overall well-being.

When we diversify, we reduce our stress levels. When you place all your ego eggs into one ego basket, you will have a greater need to perform well at that one activity to get those self-esteem points. If Venus saw herself only as a tennis player, she would feel much more pressure every time she stepped onto the court to play well and win. Venus has reduced her stress levels, however, by spreading the wealth. She can feel good about herself from her many activities. When she is not playing tennis, or not playing well, she can boost her self-esteem by designing a unique sweater for her favorite sport. With greater balance, the pressure is off for Venus to always perform well only at tennis.

The ironic point of balance is that it increases your production by taking time away. When you have many interests to give you balance, as Venus and Donald have, you will have greater levels of energy because of lower levels of stress. As a result, you will most likely produce at higher levels for longer periods of time.

Unfortunately, many people in business do not see the irony in balance. They believe it is a badge of honor to work 80 hours a week and never take a timeout, to have an outside hobby, or to go on a vacation. Lee Iacocca, of Chrysler fame, has said, "I have seen many executives who have said with pride to me, 'Boy, I worked so hard last year I did not even take a vacation.' " To Iacocca, such thinking was foolish. He believes that if you can take responsibility for an $80 million project, then you should be able to plan two weeks out of the year to have some fun.

Follow Lee Iacocca's philosophy: Be smart by adding balance. Following are tips to help you become less stressed and more productive by diversifying your life's portfolio.

BALANCE BREEDS RESILIENCY

Jack Nicklaus is more than just a great golfer. He is a husband, father, grandfather, and a business entrepreneur. The Golden Bear, as Jack is known, designs golf courses, has a golf club manufacturing business, a sports agency, and a clothing line. While some of his critics mentioned that all of these outside interests may have hurt his golf game, Jack believes it actually added to his good play by giving him a greater level of resiliency. Nicklaus has mentioned that his many family activities and business interests provided essential getaways from golf that refreshed him and renewed his eagerness for competitive golf.

Become more resilient in troubled economic times with the creation of balance in your life.

BALANCE PROMOTES HAPPINESS

Being unidimensional may lead to unhappiness, no matter how great the job. As Robert Reich describes it, being a member of President Clinton's cabinet was so much better than any job he had ever had before. However, the rest of his life was ignored. He lost contact with his old friends as well as with his wife and children.

Until one day, when he phoned for the sixth time in a row to say that he would not be home to see his young boys. His youngest son told him to wake him, even if he was desperately late, to which Robert asked why. His youngest son said, "I just want to know you were home." At that moment, Reich realized how unhappy he was being unidimensional in his life. He subsequently left his job as the Secretary of Labor at the end of President Clinton's first term.

Are you unidimensional at your job and in your life? Do you spend enough quality time with your friends and family? Are you out of balance with your job and your family?

Are you suffering from the same unhappy fate as Robert Reich?

Recall two of your happiest moments. Were they associated with your job? Enough said about being out of balance and happiness.

BALANCE PREVENTS BURNOUT

Being unidimensional can contribute to burnout. Sports psychologists have discovered that athletes who are unidimensional (played only one sport) suffered from greater burnout than those athletes who are multidimensional (played a variety of sports). When all your ego eggs are in one basket, they can crack more easily. This same principle can be applied to work.

Are you feeling drained and tired? Are you on the way to burnout? Are you suffering from unidimensionality?

Diversify your life's portfolio. Add meaningful and fulfilling activities, and your life will accrue more pleasure in the long run.

PART 7

MASTERING FULL THROTTLE

CHAPTER FIFTY-THREE

Hit It Out of the Park!

The scene was the first game of the 1988 World Series. The Los Angeles Dodgers were at bat playing the heavily favored Oakland Athletics. The famous Dodger manager, Tommy Lasorda, made a surprise move at the end of the game. He summoned Kirk Gibson to the plate as a pinch hitter. Although a great player, most experts believed that Gibson might not even suit up for this game because he was so badly bruised and battered from regular season play.

But Gibson believed that he would play, and mentally prepared himself for the game while still in the locker room. He would be facing Dennis Eckersley, the Oakland ace, and he knew him quite well because of their many encounters. Calling upon his previous positive experiences, Gibson created a vivid and realistic imagined scene with all of Eckersley's nuances. Gibson also imagined the extreme pressure of the situation, with the fans going nuts and all the cameras flashing at his every move. Yet, he still performed brilliantly.

Straight out of a Hollywood movie, Gibson limped from the dugout to the plate. It was the bottom of the ninth inning with two outs. The Dodgers were trailing 4 to 3. To add to the excitement, the count became full. All Tommy wanted from Gibson was a hit, but Gibson did more. He blasted a game-winning 2-run homer, and with that momentum, the Dodgers went on to win the series.

Kirk Gibson hit it out of the park because he mastered his emotions under pressure. He was mentally and emotionally prepared for the moment and he became a legend in baseball for it.

Are you ready, mentally and emotionally, for all the challenges you will face in this battle we call work?

More than 2,000 years ago, the philosopher Epictetus wrote that no man is free who is not a master of himself. It is my hope that this book will give you the tools to become free of fear and negativity—to become a master of your emotions. Think of this book as your guide on the journey toward excellence. Read it again and again, once may not be enough. There are many skills in this book that take time and patience to master. But once acquired, these skills will empower you to achieve at the highest level and to hit your problems and challenges out of the park again and again and again!

I leave you with these simple thoughts on your way toward excellence:

Find your passion

Create your path

Make the commitment

Enjoy the journey

ESAT (EMOTIONAL STRENGTH ASSESSMENT TOOL)

1. I know why I perform at my best.

1	2	3	4	5
Totally Disagree		Agree		Totally Agree

2. I enjoy speaking in front of my peers.

1	2	3	4	5
Totally Disagree		Agree		Totally Agree

3. I set challenging goals at work.

1	2	3	4	5
Totally Disagree		Agree		Totally Agree

4. I feel out of balance in my life.

1	2	3	4	5
Totally Agree		Agree		Totally Disagree

5. I concentrate better than my peers.

1	2	3	4	5
Totally Disagree		Agree		Totally Agree

6. I am energized every day.

1	2	3	4	5
Totally Disagree		Agree		Totally Agree

7. I am confident about my abilities.

1	2	3	4	5
Totally Disagree		Agree		Totally Agree

8. I do not know why I perform terribly on certain days.

1	2	3	4	5
Totally Agree		Agree		Totally Disagree

9. At times, I have lost my passion for my job.

1	2	3	4	5
Totally Agree		Agree		Totally Disagree

10. I do not like making mistakes.

1	2	3	4	5
Totally Agree		Agree		Totally Disagree

11. I use my strengths often.

1	2	3	4	5
Totally Disagree		Agree		Totally Agree

12. I am able to handle bad breaks.

1	2	3	4	5
Totally Disagree		Agree		Totally Agree

13. I allow pressure to get the best of me.

1	2	3	4	5
Totally Agree		Agree		Totally Disagree

14. My job is making a difference.

1	2	3	4	5
Totally Disagree		Agree		Totally Agree

15. I am often distracted.

1	2	3	4	5
Totally Agree		Agree		Totally Disagree

16. I am very creative.

1	2	3	4	5
Totally Disagree		Agree		Totally Agree

17. I focus on what I can control at work.

1	2	3	4	5
Totally Disagree		Agree		Totally Agree

18. I do not have a plan for when things go bad.

1	2	3	4	5
Totally Agree		Agree		Totally Disagree

Emotional Awareness 1, 8, 11

High = 12 or above

Med = 9 or above

Low = 6 or above

Emotional Preparedness 7, 12, 18

High = 12 or above

Med = 9 or above

Low = 6 or above

Emotional Bravado 2, 10, 13

High = 12 or above

Med = 9 or above

Low = 6 or above

Emotional Connectedness 5, 15, 16

High = 12 or above

Med = 9 or above

Low = 6 or above

Emotional Drive 3, 6, 9

High = 12 or above

Med = 9 or above

Low = 6 or above

Emotional Balance 4, 14, 17

High = 12 or above

Med = 9 or above

Low = 6 or above

BIBLIOGRAPHY

CHAPTER ONE: CYCLING WITH ENERGY

Carlson, Richard. *Don't Sweat the Small Stuff*. New York: Hyperion Books, 1997.

Israel, Paul. *Edison: A Life of Invention*. New York: John Wiley & Sons, 1998.

CHAPTER TWO: VISION GUIDES DESTINY

Berra, Yogi. *The Yogi Book*. New York: Workman Publishing, 1999.

Covey, Stephen. *Everyday Greatness*. Nashville, TN: Thomas Nelson, 2006.

Garfield, Charles. *Peak Performers*. New York: Harper Paperbacks, 1987.

Leider, Richard J. *The Power of Purpose*. San Francisco, CA: Berrett-Koehler Publishers, 2005.

Pausch, Randy, and Jeffrey Zaslow. *The Last Lecture*. New York: Hyperion Books, 2008.

Reeve, Christopher. *Nothing Is Impossible: Reflections on a New Life*. New York: Simon & Schuster Audio, 2002.

Wade, Don. *"And Then Justin told Sergio. . ."* Chicago, IL: Contemporary books, 2002.

Wilson, Larry, and Hersch Wilson. *Play to Win*. Austin, TX: Bard Press, 2004.

CHAPTER THREE: RACE INTO THE STRENGTH ZONE

Armstrong, Lance. *It's Not About the Bike*. New York: Penguin Putnam, 2000.

Buckingham, Marcus. *First, Break all the Rules*. New York: Simon and Schuster, 1999.

CHAPTER FOUR: SET YOUR FLAME

Greenspan, Bud. *Sydney 2000 Olympics: Bud Greenspan's Gold From Down Under*. Bud Greenspan, director. New York: Cappy Productions, 2001.

Dorfman, Harvey. *Coaching the Mental Game*. Lanham, MD: Taylor Trade Publishing, 2003.

Grothe, Mardy. *Oxymoronica*. New York: HarperCollins, 2004.

Jackson, Phil. *Sacred Hoops*. New York: Hyperion Books, 2001.

Lynch, Jerry, and Al Chungliang Huang. *Thinking Body, Dancing Mind*. New York: Bantam Books, 1992.

Mack, Gary. *Mind Gym*. New York: McGraw-Hill, 2002.

Steinberg, Gregg. *Mental Rules for Golf*. Nashville, TN: TowleHouse Publishing, 2003.

http://www.youtube.com/watch?v=52hsHIkDt-k.

CHAPTER FIVE: GET A CHARGE FROM RISK

Kriegel, Robert, and Louis Patler. *If it ain't broke . . . Break It!* New York: Little, Brown and Company, 1991.

Investors Business Daily. August 13, 2004.

Roosevelt, Theodore. *The Strenuous Life*. New York: The Century Company, 1902.

USA Today. September 20, 2004.

CHAPTER SIX: FIND YOUR FLOW

Steinberg, Gregg. *Mental Rules for Golf*. Nashville, TN: Towlehouse Publishing, 2003.

CHAPTER SEVEN: STICK WITH THE BASICS

Friedman, Thomas. *Longitudes and Attitudes.* New York: Farrar, Straus and Giroux, 2002.

Gwynn, Tony. *The Art of Hitting.* New York: GT Publishing, 1998.

Hill, Andrew, with John Wooden. *Be Quick—But Don't Hurry!* New York: Simon and Schuster, 2001.

Success, October 2008.

CHAPTER EIGHT: THROUGH THE UPRIGHTS

O'Donnell, Chuck. *Dempsey, Tom: The Game I Will Never Forget.* Football Digest, July-August 2003; http://findarticles.com/p/articles/mi_m0FCL/is_10_32/ai_102656419.

Los Angeles Times, October 19, 2008.

CHAPTER NINE: START WITH A BEGINNER'S MIND

Rosenthal, Robert, and Lenore Jacobson. *Pygmalion in the Classroom.* New York: Holt, Rinehart & Winston, 1968.

CHAPTER TEN: PLAN FOR THE BEST, BUT PREPARE FOR THE WORST

Murphy, Shane. *The Achievement Zone.* New York: Putnam, 1996.

Steinberg, Gregg. *Flying Lessons.* Nashville, TN: Thomas Nelson, 2007.

Steinberg, Gregg. *Mental Rules for Golf.* Nashville, TN: Towlehouse Publishing, 2003.

Verbal communication, Rudy Giuliani, October 2008.

Los Angeles Times, October 19, 2008.

CHAPTER ELEVEN: WEAR THE RED SHIRT

Loehr, James. *Stress for Success.* New York: Three Rivers Press, 1998.

CHAPTER TWELVE: CHOOSE YOUR ATTITUDE

Frankl, Victor. *Man's Search for Meaning.* Boston: Beacon Press, 1959.

Goldberg, Alan. *Sports Slump Busting.* Champaign, IL: Human Kinetics Publishers, 1997.

Steinberg, Gregg. *Flying Lessons.* Nashville, TN: Thomas Nelson, 2007.

CHAPTER THIRTEEN: FILL YOUR MIND WITH GOLDEN NUGGETS

Covey, Stephen. *Everyday Greatness.* Nashville, TN: Thomas Nelson, 2006.

Kriegel, Robert, and Louis Patler. *If it ain't broke ... Break It!* New York: Little, Brown and Company, 1991.

CHAPTER FOURTEEN: ENLIGHTEN YOUR GAME

Israel, Paul. *Edison: A Life of Invention.* New York: John Wiley & Sons, 1998.

Seligman, Martin. *Learned Optimism.* New York: Simon and Schuster, 1998.

CHAPTER FIFTEEN: BE COMFORTABLE IN THE UNCOMFORTABLE

Fortune, October 30, 2006.

Steinberg, Gregg. *Mental Rules for Golf.* Nashville, TN: Towlehouse Publishing, 2003.

CHAPTER SIXTEEN: PUMP UP WITH POSITIVE SELF-TALK

The Ultimate Athlete: Pushing the Limit, Scott Hicks, director. Discovery Channel Pictures, 1996.

Garfield, Charles. *Peak Performance.* Boston: Houghton Mifflin, 1984.

Robbins, Tony. *Awaken the Giant Within.* New York: Simon and Schuster, 1992.

CHAPTER SEVENTEEN: GET A LIFELINE

Hershiser, Orel, and Robert Wolgemuth. *Between the Lines: Nine Principles to Live By.* New York: Warner Books, 2001.

McEnroe, John. *You Cannot Be Serious.* New York: Berkley Trade, 2003.

CHAPTER EIGHTEEN: THINK BIG

Riach, Steve. *Amazing Athletes, Amazing Moments.* Kansas City, MO: Hallmark Gift Books, 2005.

CHAPTER NINETEEN: ANTICIPATE YOUR EXCELLENCE

Sports Illustrated, 1993.

Feller, Bob. *Bob Feller's Little Black Book of Baseball Wisdom.* New York: Contemporary Books, 2001.

Steinberg, Gregg, and Robert Singer. *Mental Quickness Training.* DVD, 1995.

CHAPTER TWENTY: SQUASH THE GRAPES

Pausch, Randy, and Jeffrey Zaslow. *The Last Lecture.* New York: Hyperion Books, 2008.

CHAPTER TWENTY-TWO: FACE YOUR FEARS

Covey, Stephen. *Everyday Greatness.* Nashville, TN: Thomas Nelson, 2006.

Goleman, Daniel, and Richard Boyatzis. "Social intelligence and the Biology of Leadership." *Harvard Business Review,* September 2008.

Maxwell, John. *Failing Forward.* Nashville, TN: Thomas Nelson, 2000.

The Tennessean, October 2008.

CHAPTER TWENTY-THREE: SING THE CARLY PRINCIPLE

Marie Claire, November 2008.

Los Angeles Times, October 19, 2008.

Steinberg, Gregg. *Mental Rules for Golf.* Nashville, TN: Towlehouse Publishing, 2003.

Thomas, Marlo. *The Right Words at the Right Time.* New York: Atria Books, 2004.

CHAPTER TWENTY-FOUR: GET RATIONAL

Greenberg, Jerold. *Comprehensive Stress Management.* New York: McGraw-Hill, 2004.

Kriegel, Robert. *How to Succeed in Business Without Working So Damn Hard.* New York: Warner Books, 2002.

CHAPTER TWENTY-FIVE: MAKE GOOD FROM BAD

Fortune, October 30, 2006.

Dorfman, Harvey. *The Mental Game of Baseball.* South Bend, IN: Diamond Communications, 1989.

Investor's Business Daily, October 4, 2004.

CHAPTER TWENTY-SIX: RISK THE PAIN OF LOSING

Steinberg, Gregg. *Mental Rules for Golf.* Nashville, TN: Towlehouse Publishing, 2003.

CHAPTER TWENTY-EIGHT: DEVELOP POSITIVE RITUALS

Coop, Richard, and Bill Fields. *Mind Over Golf.* New York: MacMillan, 1993.

Loehr, James. *Stress for Success.* New York: Three Rivers Press, 1998.

CHAPTER TWENTY-NINE: KICK THE ANXIETY HABIT

Andrisani, John, *Think Like Tiger.* New York: Putnam, 2002.

Bradley, Bill. *Values of the Game.* New York: Artisan, 1998.

CHAPTER THIRTY: ZEN AND THE ART OF BUSINESS

Hanh, Thich Nhat. *Peace Is Every Step.* New York: Bantam, 1991.

Jackson, Phil. *Sacred Hoops: Spiritual Lessons of a Hardwood Warrior*. New York: Hyperion Books, 1995.

Lowe, Janet. *Michael Jordan Speaks*. New York: John Wiley & Sons, 1999.

Success, October 2008.

CHAPTER THIRTY-ONE: QUIET THE MIND

Covey, Stephen. *Everyday Greatness*. Nashville, TN: Thomas Nelson, 2006.

Ed Catmull. "How Pixar Fosters Collective Creativity." *Harvard Business Review*, September 2008.

The Ultimate Athlete: Pushing the Limit, Scott Hicks, director. Discovery Channel Pictures, 1996.

Steinberg, Gregg. *Flying Lessons*. Nashville, TN: Thomas Nelson, 2007.

CHAPTER THIRTY-TWO: DEVELOP A POST-EVENT ROUTINE

Loehr, James. *Stress for Success*. New York: Three Rivers Press, 1998.

CHAPTER THIRTY-FOUR: FLOW WITH YOUR CONCENTRATION STYLE

Weinberg, Robert, and Daniel Gould. *Foundations of Sport and Exercise Psychology*. Champaign, IL: Human Kinetics Publishers, 2007.

CHAPTER THIRTY-FIVE: DO THE TWAIN

Naber, John. *Awaken the Olympian Within*. Santa Ana, CA: Griffin Publishing, 1999.

Wenger, Win, and Richard Poe. *The Einstein Factor*. New York: Gramercy Books, 2004.

CHAPTER THIRTY-SIX: PASSION PLAY— THE PHELPSIAN WAY

Harvard Business Review, September 2008.

Investor's Business Daily, November 2004.

CHAPTER THIRTY-SEVEN: DISCOVER THE POWER OF PRIDE

Greenspan, Bud. *Salt Lake 2002: Bud Greenspan's Favorite Stories of Olympic Glory.* Bud Greenspan, director. New York: Cappy Productions, 2002.
The Tennessean, August 24, 2008.

CHAPTER THIRTY-EIGHT: THE SECRET IS IN THE DIRT

Bradley, Bill. *Values of the Game.* Broadway Books, 1998.
Steinberg, Gregg. *Mental Rules for Golf.* Nashville, TN: Towlehouse Publishing, 2003.

CHAPTER THIRTY-NINE: FIND YOUR JOY SPOT

Steinberg, Gregg. *Mental Rules for Golf.* Nashville, TN: Towlehouse Publishing, 2003.

CHAPTER FORTY: GET A MENTOR

Film at Louisville Slugger at Louisville, KY.
Gelb, Michael. *How to Think Like Leonardo da Vinci.* New York: Dell Publishing, 1998.
King, Billie Jean. *Pressure Is a Privilege.* New York: Lifetime Media, 2008.
Sobel, David. S., and Robert Ornstein. "Good Humor, Good Health." Los Altos, CA: Institute for the Study of Human Knowledge. Adapted from *The Healthy Mind, Healthy Body Handbook.* Los Altos, CA: DRx, 1996.
Los Angeles Times, September 2008.

CHAPTER FORTY-ONE: DRIVE TO THE GOAL

60 Minutes, New York: CBS News, November 9, 2008.

CHAPTER FORTY-TWO: COMMIT TO FINISHING THE RACE

Riach, Steve. *Amazing Athletes, Amazing Moments.* Kansas City, MO: Hallmark Gift Books, 2005.

CHAPTER FORTY-THREE: ROCKET PAST A PLATEAU

Insel, Paul, and Walton Roth. *Core Concepts in Health*, 9th ed. Boston: McGraw-Hill, 2002.

Staff of USA Today. *Michael Phelps, the World's Greatest Olympian.* New York: Triumph Books, 2008.

CHAPTER FORTY-FOUR: CATAPULT WITH CHARITY

ABC News, Los Angeles, May 2008.

CHAPTER FORTY-FIVE: LEAP ABOVE BOREDOM

Barber, Tiki. *Tiki: My Life in the Game and Beyond.* New York: Simon Spotlight Entertainment, 2007.

Kriegel, Robert. *The C Zone.* New York: Anchor Books, 1984.

Seligman, Martin. *Authentic Happiness.* New York: Free Press, 2002.

Woods, Earl. *Training a Tiger.* New York: Collins Living, 1997.

http://www.youtube.com/watch?v=3fsDaYFcHI0&feature=related

CHAPTER FORTY-SEVEN: LET IT BE

Thomas, Marlo. *The Right Words at the Right Time.* New York: Atria Books, 2004.

CHAPTER FORTY-EIGHT: SERENITY NOW

Steinberg, Gregg. *Mental Rules for Golf.* Nashville, TN: Towlehouse Publishing, 2003.

CHAPTER FORTY-NINE: THE BEST ARE NEVER SATISFIED

Covey, Stephen. *Everyday Greatness.* Nashville, TN: Thomas Nelson, 2000.

Dorfman, Harvey. *The Mental Game of Baseball.* South Bend, IN: Diamond Communications, 1989.

Hamm, Mia. *Go for the Goal.* New York: Harper Paperbacks, 2000.

Kriegel, Robert. *If it ain't broke … Break It.* New York: Warner Books, 1991.

Williams, Ted. *My Turn at Bat.* New York: Simon and Schuster, 1969.

CHAPTER FIFTY: LET INTEGRITY FLOW

Busbee, David. Yahoo Sports. November 19, 2008.

Covey, Stephen. *Everyday Greatness.* Nashville, TN: Thomas Nelson, 2000.

King, Billie Jean. *Pressure Is a Privilege.* New York: Lifetime Media, 2008.

Yeh, Raymond. *The Art of Business.* Olathe, CO: Zero Time Publishing, 2004.

CHAPTER FIFTY-ONE: TEMPER COMPETITIVENESS WITH MASTERY

King, Billie Jean. *Pressure Is a Privilege.* New York: Lifetime Media, 2008.

Steinberg, Gregg. *Flying Lessons.* Nashville, TN: Thomas Nelson, 2007.

Steinberg, Gregg. *Multiple Goal Orientations.* Dissertation Abstracts, 1996.

CHAPTER FIFTY-TWO: DIVERSIFY YOUR LIFE'S PORTFOLIO

Covey, Stephen. *Everyday Greatness.* Nashville, TN: Thomas Nelson, 2000.

BRING DR. GREGG STEINBERG TO YOUR ORGANIZATION. HE IS HERE FOR YOU. . . .

Dedicated to helping people become more effective at work and happier in life, he has devised the following two seminars:

Full Throttle: How to Supercharge Your Energy and Performance at Work

This seminar brings the book, *Full Throttle*, to life! You will learn additional secrets to mastering your emotions through the development of the 6 key emotional strengths. Accelerate your way to excellence with this seminar.

Here is what to expect to achieve:

- Get charged up for every client
- Get more focused for every meeting and every phone call
- Develop greater balance in your life
- Become more productive but work less hard
- Plug up all the energy drains from work and life
- Discover that inner flame for excellence

Bring Dr. Gregg Steinberg to your organization! Please call 931-206-1328 or e-mail Mentalrules24@msn.com for scheduling. Go to www.DrGreggSteinberg.com to learn more.

Full Throttle Leadership: How to Supercharge Your Employees

This seminar applies the book, *Full Throttle*, to leadership. You will learn the skills and tools for supercharging your staff and employees in all situations. Help your people become more successful and happier.

256

Here is what to expect to achieve from your staff:

- Higher levels of production
- Less burnout
- Better attitude
- More creativity
- Greater motivation

Bring Dr. Gregg Steinberg to your organization! Please call 931-206-1328 or e-mail Mentalrules24@msn.com for scheduling. Go to www.DrGreggSteinberg.com for more information.

Dr. Gregg Steinberg is an award-winning speaker who is known for his dynamic and entertaining presentational style. He provides audiences with hands-on tools and powerful ideas. Make your next event extraordinary!

IF YOU WOULD LIKE MORE INFORMATION AND TIPS, PLEASE GO TO....

www.DrGreggSteinberg.com

At this site you can.....

1. Get *Full Throttle* CDs and DVD's
2. Receive a free *Full Throttle* newsletter
3. Develop your own personalized coaching program with Dr. Gregg
4. Get other great free stuff

Read More Books by Dr. Gregg:

Flying Lessons: 122 Strategies to soar into life with competence and confidence (Thomas Nelson, 2007). This book gives parents hands-on tools and great tips to help their children succeed in any field! Please visit www.DrGregg Steinberg.com for your autographed copy.

Mentalrules for Golf (Towlehouse, 2003). This book gives you the secrets to develop mental and emotional toughness for the golf course and life. Please visit www.mentalrules .com or www.DrGreggSteinberg.com for your autographed copy.